CHATTANOOGA

The Renaissance of a City

CHATTANOOGA

The Renaissance of a City

PHILLIP G. STEVENS with Linda Chase and Fiona Soltes

Left: 1891 Dome Building, downtown. Center and right: At Chickamauga and Chattanooga National Military Park, a Civil War reenactment and the Memorial to the Battle of Chattanooga

CPG *cherbo* publishing group, inc.

president	JACK C. CHERBO
chief operating officer	ELAINE HOFFMAN
editorial director	CHRISTINA M. BEAUSANG
managing feature editor	MARGARET L. MARTIN
senior profiles editor	J. KELLEY YOUNGER
profiles editor	LIZA YETENEKIAN SMITH
associate editors	SYLVIA EMRICH-TOMA
	JENNY KORNFELD
editorial assistant/proofreader	MARK K. NISHIMURA
profiles writers	B. D. CAMPBELL
	SYLVIA EMRICH-TOMA
	TERRI JONISCH
	JO ELLEN KRUMM
	TERRAN LAMP
	RODD MONTS
	BENJAMIN PROST
	ERICA RHEINSCHILD
creative director	PERI A. HOLGUIN
senior designer	THEODORE E. YEAGER
designer	NELSON CAMPOS
senior photo editor	WALTER MLADINA
photo editor	KAREN MAZE
digital color specialist	ART VASQUEZ
sales administrator	JOAN K. BAKER
client services supervisor	PATRICIA DE LEONARD
senior client services coordinator	LESLIE E. SHAW
client services coordinator	KENYA HICKS
executive assistant	JUDY ROBITSCHEK
administrative assistant	BILL WAY
eastern regional manager	MARCIA WEISS
regional development manager	GLEN EDWARDS
publisher's representative	JEANNE SCHEDEL

Cherbo Publishing Group, Inc.
Encino, California 91316
© 2008 by Cherbo Publishing Group, Inc.
All rights reserved. Published 2008.

Printed in Canada
By Friesens

Subsidiary Production Office
Santa Rosa, CA, USA
888.340.6049

Library of Congress Cataloging-in-Publication data
Stevens, Phillip G., Linda Chase, and Fiona Soltes
A pictorial guide highlighting Chattanooga's
economic and social advantages.

Library of Congress Control Number 2008922915
ISBN 978-1-882933-86-0
Visit the CPG Web site at www.cherbopub.com.

The information in this publication is the most recent available, has been carefully researched to ensure accuracy, and has been reviewed by the sponsor. Cherbo Publishing Group, Inc. cannot and does not guarantee either the correctness of all information furnished it or the complete absence of errors, including omissions.

To purchase additional copies of this book, contact Joan Baker at Cherbo Publishing Group: jbaker@cherbopub.com or phone 818.783.0040 ext. 27.

Dedication and Acknowledgments

This book is dedicated to the man who made the greatest impact in my life. Although he was aware of this project from its conception and was proud and excited to see its completion, he did not live to see it published. I know that his pride and excitement lives in its publication. In loving memory of my dad, Carl L. Stevens Sr.

While exploring Chattanooga during my research, I was constantly reminded of why I fell in love with Chattanooga, and when discovering things that I was unaware of, I fell in love with Chattanooga even more.

I am grateful to each of the following for their individual expertise, contribution, or support: Matt Lea, J. Ed Marston, Jo Crawley, Sarah Beth Schenck, Karen and Mark Timon, Randy Ridge, Ed Graham, Dennis Tate, Anne Benton, Jerry D. Pearson, Mike Rose, Alan Colbert, Sam and Sandy Condra, Anna Cotton, Melody Farwell, Brad Kennedy, Connie Pauley, Mark Keil, and Liz Henley. I thank you for your support and friendship.

This book would not have been possible had it not been for Margaret Martin with Cherbo Publishing Group. I am most appreciative for her knowledge, her support, and her friendship. And to Michelle Michaud, thank you for the support and for the confidence you had in me.

To my family: my mother, Mary Stevens, and my brother, Steve Stevens, I am not only thankful for your support but in awe of the unconditional love. God bless you.

Lastly, thank you to the people of Chattanooga, both past and present. Chattanooga has that strong sense of community that larger cities cannot duplicate, and I found it in the details during my research. It truly is her people who have enriched and molded a community worth calling "home." Thank you!—*Phillip G. Stevens*

Market Street Bridge (also known as the John Ross Bridge) (left) and Walnut Street Bridge

The transformation of Chattanooga's riverfront, with major enhancements to the Tennessee Aquarium, the Hunter Museum of American Art and the Creative Discovery Museum, occurred because of the generosity of those who gave to the 21st Century Waterfront Trust. Led by the City of Chattanooga, and without the use of the city's general funds, the massive project, from an idea to full implementation, was completed in just 27 months. This tremen...

AmSouth Bank

Ross's Landing

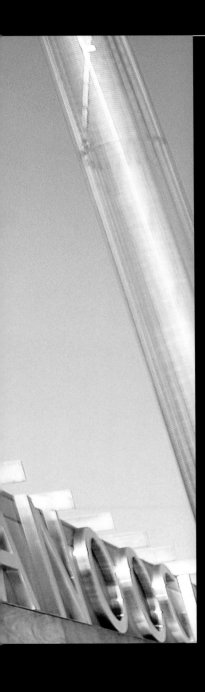

TABLE OF CONTENTS

CHATTANOOGA TIMELINE   2

PART ONE   6
SOUTHERN COMFORT:
AT WORK, AT HOME, AND AT PLAY IN CHATTANOOGA

CHAPTER ONE
NATURAL ATTRACTION: Quality of Life
by Phillip G. Stevens   8

CHAPTER TWO
MADE IN CHATTANOOGA: Manufacturing and Food Processing
by Fiona Soltes   28

CHAPTER THREE
MIND AND BODY: Education and Health Care
by Linda Chase   40

CHAPTER FOUR
A FOUNDATION FOR SUCCESS: Professional and Consumer Services
by Fiona Soltes   52

CHAPTER FIVE
MAKING CONNECTIONS: Transportation, Energy, and Telecommunications
by Linda Chase   64

PART TWO   76
SUCCESS STORIES:
PROFILES OF COMPANIES AND ORGANIZATIONS

PHOTO CREDITS   140

Left to right: East African crowned crane at the Chattanooga Zoo; Creative Discovery Museum; Ruby Falls

Left to right: Southern stingray in the Gulf of Mexico exhibit at the Tennessee Aquarium; the Plaza at the aquarium

Left to right: The Impressions performing with the Chattanooga Symphony and Opera; hammer-dulcimer player at Rock City; musician Rebecca Jean Smith playing at a downtown event

Left to right: Biking in the Great Smoky Mountains; downtown yoga class; wakeboarding at the city's waterfront

CORPORATIONS &
ORGANIZATIONS PROFILED

The following organizations have made a valuable commitment to the quality of this publication. The City of Chattanooga gratefully acknowledges their participation in *Chattanooga: The Renaissance of a City.*

BlueCross BlueShield of Tennessee, Inc. . . . . .xx, 96–97

CBL & Associates Properties, Inc. .85

Chattanooga Choo Choo 106–07

Chattanooga Manufacturers Association 129

Comcast Cable Communications, Inc. . . . . xx, 132–35

Cornerstone Community Bank . . . . .xx, 80–81

Covenant College 90

Double-Cola Co.–USA 120–21

East Tech Company . . . . xx, 118–19

EPB 136

Erlanger Health System 102–03

ERMC 84

Hamilton Plastics, Inc. 116–17

Hazlett, Lewis & Bieter, PLLC 126–27

Heil Environmental . . . . .xx, 112–13

Joseph Decosimo and Company, PLLC 128

McKee Foods Corporation . . . . .xx, 114–15

Memorial Health Care System . . . . .xx, 100–01

Propex Inc. . . . . .xx, 110–11

Sofix Corporation 122

Southern Adventist University 88–89

Unum . . . . .xx, 94–95

Hunter Museum of American Art

BUSINESS VISIONARIES

The following companies and organizations are recognized as innovators in their fields and have played a prominent role in this publication, as they have in the city.

 **of Tennessee**
plans for better health. plans for a better life.™

BlueCross BlueShield of Tennessee, Inc.
801 Pine Street, Chattanooga, TN 37402
Kathy Reid Papson, Manager, Talent Acquisition
Phone: 423-535-5226 / Fax: 423-535-5792
E-mail: kathy_reid-papson@bcbst.com
Web site: www.bcbst.com

Comcast Cable Corporation
2030 East Polymer Drive, Chattanooga, TN 37421
Valerie Gillespie, Vice President and General Manager
Phone: 423-855-4300 / Fax: 423-855-4237
Web site: www.comcast.com

BUILDING STRONG FINANCIAL FOUNDATIONS
Member FDIC

Cornerstone Community Bank
Corporate Headquarters: 835 Georgia Avenue, Chattanooga, TN 37402
Mailing Address: 6401 Lee Highway, Suite B, Chattanooga, TN 37421
Phone: 423-385-3000
E-mail: customerservice@cscb-chatt.com
Web site: www.cscbank.com

East Tech Company Inc.
767 River Terminal Road, Chattanooga, TN 37406
Phone: 423-624-2550 / Fax: 423-624-2552
Web site: www.easttechcompany.com

THE WHEELS ARE ALWAYS TURNING
A DOVER COMPANY

Heil Environmental
5751 Cornelison Road, Chattanooga, TN 37411
Contact: Mark Guild, Director of Marketing
Phone: 866-367-4345 / Fax: 423-855-3478
E-mail: corp@heil.com
Web site: www.heil.com
"The Wheels Are Always Turning"

McKee
Foods
Corporation

McKee Foods Corporation
P.O. Box 750, Collegedale, TN 37315
Contact: Mike Gloekler, Corporate Communications and Public Relations Manager
Phone: 423-238-7111 ext. 22440 / Fax: 423-238-7127
E-mail: mike_gloekler@mckee.com
Web site: www.mckeefoods.com

† CATHOLIC HEALTH INITIATIVES
Memorial Health Care System

Memorial Hospital • Memorial North Park Hospital

The power of faith and excellence

Memorial Health Care System
2525 de Sales Avenue, Chattanooga, TN 37404
Phone: 423-495-2525
Web site: www.memorial.org
"The Power of Faith and Excellence"

PROPEX®

THE ADVANTAGE CREATORS.™

Propex Inc.
6025 Lee Highway, Suite 425, Chattanooga, TN 37421
Contact: Dan Alderman, Marketing Coordinator
Phone: 423-553-2116 / Fax: 423-553-2109
Web site: www.propexinc.com
"The Advantage Creators."

Unum Group
One Fountain Square, Chattanooga, TN 37402
Contact: Jim Sabourin, Vice President, Corporate Communications
Phone: 800-635-5597 / Fax: 423-294-3962
E-mail: Corpcomm@unum.com
Web site: www.unum.com
"Better Benefits at Work."

Sunset atop Lookout Mountain

Left to right: Chattanooga Ballet; Chattanooga Symphony and Opera (CSO) production of *Rigoletto*; CSO in concert

Left to right: The Passage at Ross's Landing; water feature at base of the Passage

Left to right: Chattanooga Traditional Jazz Festival at the Chattanooga Choo Choo hotel; Coolidge Park carousel; South Korean dance troupe at the Riverbend Festival

Celebrating the grand reopening of century-old City Hall

Welcome,

It is a privilege and an honor to welcome you on behalf of the City of Chattanooga to *Chattanooga: The Renaissance of a City*. As you turn the pages, you will see that Chattanooga is an exciting and beautiful city with a rich historical past.

Chattanooga became a city just over 150 years ago. What was once a small Indian village has now become one of *U.S. News and World Report*'s top "Best Cities in the world" in which to live, work, or play.

This book will highlight some of our many family attractions, from natural to man-made, including the Tennessee Aquarium, Ruby Falls, Rock City, the Incline Railway, Chattanooga Choo Choo, Lookout Mountain Civil War Battlefield, and the newly created Moccasin Bend National Park.

Chattanooga is famous for its rich industrial and Civil War heritage. Our beautifully transformed Downtown Riverfront highlights our Cherokee Indian heritage and our early source of major transportation, the Tennessee River. Chattanoogans are committed to education and continuing our economic viability and growth.

Whether it's a vacation destination, home or business relocation, or conference location you're looking for, Chattanooga is the place for you! Depending on your business and family travel needs, we boast numerous modes of easily accessible transportation choices including river access, three major national interstate connections, railway, and the completely full-service, state-of-the-art Chattanooga Metropolitan Airport to meet your shipping or travel needs.

On behalf of the City of Chattanooga, I would like to cordially invite you and your family to visit our wonderful Scenic City! As you will see from the pages of this book, Chattanooga is an amazing city full of history, rich cultural diversity, world-famous attractions, and southern hospitality.

We hope you will visit us soon!

Sincerely,

Ron Littlefield
Mayor

CHATTANOOGA TIMELINE

1815   1858   1867

Chief John Ross

1815 John Ross, a Cherokee chief, and Timothy Meigs open a trading post on the Tennessee River and name the area Ross's Landing.

1838 Extricated by the government, the Cherokee head west from Ross's Landing on a journey that will become known as the Trail of Tears.

1850 The Memphis and Charleston Railroad is completed; its presence will contribute to a 60 percent increase in Chattanooga's population.

Union Station, circa 1924

1858 The state of Georgia builds Union Station on 9th Street between Chestnut Street and Railroad Avenue; in 1892 Railroad Avenue will be renamed Broad Street.

1860 With a population of 2,000, Chattanooga is now considered a mid-sized city.

1863 Union and Confederate forces fight for control of Chattanooga, the "Gateway to the Deep South." The Confederates are victorious at nearby Chickamauga in September, but in November Grant's forces will defeat the Confederate army of General Braxton Bragg. The South would never recover from the loss of Chattanooga.

1867 In a disastrous flood, waters rise to a record 56.8 feet, washing away the city's only bridge over the Tennessee River; the city will remain without a bridge until 1891, when the Walnut Street Bridge is built.

1867 The Chattanooga National Cemetery is created; it is the first national cemetery to open.

1867 The First Congregationalist Church of Chattanooga becomes the first church in the South to welcome both African-American and Caucasian members.

Battle of Chattanooga, 1863

Ernest Holmes Company tow truck, circa 1920

1895 On November 16 the Incline Railway opens, taking visitors to the top of Lookout Mountain at an incline of 72.7 percent; it will remain the steepest passenger incline train in the world and a major Chattanooga attraction.

1878 The Yellow Fever Epidemic hits Chattanooga, killing 366.

1890 Chickamauga and Chattanooga National Military Park—the first national military park in the United States—opens.

Municipal Building (City Hall), circa 1910

1899 The worst snowstorm in more than 100 years hits Chattanooga.

1908 City Hall celebrates the laying of cornerstone for the new city municipal building at Lindsay and 11th streets.

1916 Chattanooga native Ernest Holmes Sr. invents the tow truck.

1917 On March 7, a second great flood inundates the city as the Tennessee River overflows its banks.

1923 Chattanooga native Bessie Smith, "Empress of the Blues," makes her recording debut with "Down Hearted Blues" on Columbia Records and sells an estimated 800,000 copies, making Smith the most successful African-American performer of her time.

Bessie Smith, circa 1920

CHATTANOOGA TIMELINE

1925   1941   1950   1957

Tennessee Valley Authority dam construction, circa 1933

Tom Thumb Golf Course, circa 1927

1950 Natural gas arrives in Chattanooga via underground piping; its availability sparks a boom for Chattanooga, and the consumption of natural gas increases by 2,500 percent.

1957 Emmy award–winning actor Leslie Jordan is born in Chattanooga.

1925 Garnet Carter sets up a miniature putting green on Lookout Mountain, experimenting with pipes and rocks, on a small course, and Tom Thumb miniature golf is born; the sport will quickly become a national craze.

1930 The first baseball game is played at Engel Stadium on April 15.

1933 On May 18, President Franklin Delano Roosevelt signs the federal act creating the Tennessee Valley Authority.

1941 Chattanooga receives special notoriety with the fame of the Glenn Miller Orchestra's big band hit, "Chattanooga Choo-Choo;" it becomes the first gold record.

1948 Chattanooga becomes the first major southern city to have African-American police officers.

Cooking with gas, Chattanooga High School, 1950

1960 History is made on a Friday afternoon in February when a small group of Howard High School students holds a sit-in at a downtown five-and-dime store lunch counter, a move that in other cities had only been done by college students.

1961   **1982**   **1995**

1995 The International Towing and Recovery Museum and Hall of Fame, the world's only museum dedicated to the towing industry, opens.

2004 The historic Read House hotel completes a $10 million renovation.

1982 In an effort to revitalize the riverfront and downtown areas of Chattanooga, the Vision 2000 project is developed.

2005 A multimillion-dollar waterfront revitalization project is completed.

1961 Preserving Chattanooga's pride in its railroad heritage, a group of Chattanoogans form the Tennessee Valley Railroad Museum.

1993 The Walnut Street Bridge reopens; at the time, it is the world's longest pedestrian bridge.

2007 City Hall reopens after undergoing a $12 million renovation, in time for its centennial.

1969 Chattanooga earns the dubious title of America's dirtiest city from the Environmental Protection Agency, prompting city officials and citizens alike to begin what will be a series of clean-up programs.

1976 Miller Park opens.

Tennessee Valley Railroad Museum

Revitalized downtown Chattanooga

City Hall centennial celebration, 2007

PART ONE
SOUTHERN COMFORT:
AT WORK, AT HOME, AND AT PLAY IN CHATTANOOGA

CHAPTER ONE

NATURAL ATTRACTION
Quality of Life

Chattanooga's identity is indelibly linked to the river that runs through it. The Tennessee's myriad twists and turns mirror the city's changing fortunes over the past two centuries. In the last 20 years, Chattanooga has undergone a true renaissance, earning it the nickname "Scenic City of the South." But Chattanooga is more than just a pretty face. It has both brains and beauty, a dynamic business environment blended with stunning natural and man-made scenery.

River Town

At the southern end of the Cumberland Plateau, surrounded by the Appalachian Mountains, Chattanooga was for thousands of years on a path traveled by the Paleo Indians and later by the Creeks and the Cherokees and by European traders. It was a Cherokee chief, John Ross, who with partner Timothy Meigs established a trading post in 1815 on a bend in the Tennessee River. Called Ross's Landing, the site soon became a thriving center of commerce. To gain autonomy over this valuable real estate, both the state and federal governments forced the Cherokee to leave the area. Their mass removal, beginning in May 1838, became known as "Nunna daul Tsuny," or the "Trail Where They Cried," more famously known as the "Trail of Tears." In 1839 the state of Tennessee incorporated the area and changed its name to Chattanooga.

The natural features of the region made it a suitable crossroads not only for river traffic but for rail traffic too. The first train of the Western & Atlantic Railroad arrived in 1849, and other rail lines soon followed, making Chattanooga a major transportation hub. After the Civil War, the city became a center for steel and iron production, earning it the nickname "the Pittsburgh of the South." But the southern city suffered many of the same problems as those of its northern counterpart, including pollution and flooding. The latter was solved through the construction of the Chickamauga Dam, a Tennessee Valley Authority project, in 1940. Pollution, however, continued, culminating in 1969 with Chattanooga's being named America's most polluted city. By the 1980s what had once been a thriving industrial and transportation site had become a rundown eyesore.

Chattanoogans, however, would not give up on their city—nor would long-time corporate residents BlueCross BlueShield of Tennessee, Erlanger Health System, the University of Tennessee at Chattanooga, Unum, and others who maintained offices here despite the hard times. Both private and public sectors joined forces in 1984 to create a program that would revive the city and reveal its hidden beauty and potential. The program, called Vision 2000, was an ambitious redevelopment plan that would transform Chattanooga into a vibrant, livable, award-winning community and earn it the nickname "Scenic City of the South."

Vision 2000 called for $12 million in investments in infrastructure and amenities in order to attract both business and residents to downtown Chattanooga. These funds were eventually leveraged into $1.5 billion in developments. New office space, residential properties, and cultural and entertainment amenities revitalized downtown. The spectacular Tennessee Aquarium, the city's signature building, was completed in 1992 and was followed by a new children's museum, an IMAX theater, and AT&T Field for the city's Double-A baseball team. One of Vision 2000's goals was to make Chattanooga a pedestrian-friendly city. The Walnut Street Bridge was converted into a pedestrian bridge connecting both sides of the 22-mile-long Tennessee Riverpark. The park itself contains 10 miles of riverside greenways for walking, hiking, and biking. A free electric shuttle (one of the largest fleets of its kind in the country) was inaugurated to whisk people around downtown without polluting the environment. Building on the success of Vision 2000 was the 21st Century Waterfront development plan, a $120 million project conceived in 2002 which planned for additional downtown housing, a marina, promenades lined with public art, and a revised traffic plan that would ease congestion. In addition, historic buildings—including City Hall—were restored to their original beauty or converted to office or residential space. The result is a city with a heart, a thriving, exciting center of commerce and culture, where Chattanoogans enjoy an unsurpassed quality of life.

And the world has taken notice. Delegations from around the nation and around the world have come to Chattanooga to learn how they can adapt Chattanooga's plans to their own needs. The city has received recognition from the American Society of Landscape Architects, the International Downtown Association, the American Planning Association, and many other respected organizations. In 1996 the United Nations honored Chattanooga with its "Best Practices" award given to 12 cities around the world. The award recognizes cities that have made marked improvements in their living environments and that promote sustainability. In 2007 Expansion Management magazine named Chattanooga one of "America's 50 Hottest Cities" for expansion.

Enterprise South Industrial Park presents an exciting opportunity for businesses considering a move to Chattanooga. The 1,600-acre site (with an additional 1,400 acres under development) is zoned for heavy industrial and manufacturing use and is certified as a megasite, making it ideal for automotive manufacturing. The groundbreaking took place in January 2003, and the third phase of development was completed in 2006. Enterprise South is within 150 miles of what is being called the Southeast Growth Corridor, which includes Knoxville, Nashville, Atlanta, and Birmingham, and is within two days' drive of 80 percent of the U.S. population.

This page: One of downtown's many new condominium developments. Opposite page: Dr. David C. Seaberg, dean of UTC's College of Medicine, reviewing patient information with Dr. Roopa Vemireddy at Erlanger Health System's Baroness Campus.

Location is just one of the Chattanooga area's many advantages. Businesses may also work with research and development centers such as the University of Tennessee's SimCenter in Chattanooga and the Arnold Engineer Development Corporation in Tullahoma, Tennessee. Chattanooga is just 100 miles from Huntsville, Alabama, home of the NASA–Marshall Space Flight Center and the Redstone Army Arsenal, and just over 100 miles from the Oak Ridge National Laboratories in Oak Ridge, Tennessee. In addition, Chattanooga has low utility rates and a highly skilled workforce of nearly half a million people.

Entrepreneurs benefit not only from the amenities the city has to offer but from incentives. Chattanooga is one of only two cities in the state eligible for Renewal Community federal tax deductions. One recipient of such a tax break is FedEx, which plans to open a FedEx Ground distribution facility on the site of a former foundry in September 2008. BlueCross BlueShield of Tennessee will open its new corporate headquarters in downtown's Cameron Hill area in 2009. In fact, tax incentives led to $300 million in investments in Chattanooga between 2002 and 2007.

So Nice to Come Home To

While Chattanoogans recognize the importance of a healthy business environment to a city's growth, they also appreciate the need for building livable communities; and building they are, with no fewer than 25 developers having projects in various stages of development in March 2007. Ample and diverse housing means there is something for all lifestyles, from singles just starting out to families to retirees. North Chattanooga and the Brainerd neighborhood feature charming bungalows, while historical neighborhoods like Fort Wood offer magnificent antebellum mansions. In Lookout Valley and Ooltewah are numerous new developments. New condominiums, town homes, lofts, and apartments are attracting people to settle downtown. Many of these developments are along the riverfront and involve conversions of historic old buildings, helping to maintain Chattanooga's ties with its past. In addition, older neighborhoods are receiving a new lease on life through revitalization programs.

Housing costs in Chattanooga are comparatively low; the median home price in August 2007 was $135,300, nearly 40 percent lower than the national average, making home ownership in Chattanooga a reality. Low- to moderate-income residents may receive assistance from the Chattanooga Neighborhood Enterprise, a nonprofit organization that develops, manages, and finances housing throughout Hamilton County and also helps with maintenance and emergency repairs.

Living Well

Chattanooga's fine quality of life is further enhanced by the presence of renowned medical facilities, known for their innovative teaching, caring staff, and cutting-edge practices.

The Erlanger Health System has five campuses, including the region's only pediatric emergency center, at T. C. Thompson Children's Hospital, and its only Level 1 trauma center. At Erlanger's Emergency Heart and Stroke Center, revolutionary breakthroughs in stroke treatment have placed the hospital at the international forefront in treating "brain attacks." Founded more than a century ago, Erlanger continues to break ground with new, less-invasive ways to treat heart and vascular diseases and to transplant kidneys, among other leading-edge medical advances.

Chattanoogans also benefit from specialty services provided by Parkridge Medical Center, which include oncology, hematology, cardiology, neurology, and more at the Sarah Cannon Cancer Center. Parkridge is also renowned for its sports medicine program. Parkridge East Hospital offers a women's center, a neonatal intensive care unit, a center for the diagnosis and treatment of sleep disorders, and a spine and orthopedic center. At Parkridge Valley, children, adolescents, and adults receive treatment for behavioral disorders and addictions.

Memorial Health Care System, the region's only faith-based health care system, has two acute-care hospitals and multiple facilities serving the community. With advanced technology, expertise, and comprehensive resources, Memorial is a regional leader in cardiac, cancer, orthopedic, and surgical care. In 2006 it was recognized as one of the Top 100 Hospitals in America and as a Top 100 Heart Hospital by Thomson Healthcare, a respected research and analysis company.

Lessons in Success

In the area of education, Chattanooga is committed to providing opportunities for academic and vocational achievement for students of all ages.

Chattanooga's public schools are administered by the Hamilton County Department of Education, which oversees 78 elementary and secondary schools and more than 40,000 students. Close to 12,000 students attend the 16 high schools, 9,500 are enrolled in the 21 middle schools, and some 18,500 children attend the 41 elementary schools. There are 16 magnet schools offering special programs in fine and performing arts, environmental sciences, science and technology, museum studies, and technical and vocational training. Some of the county schools partner with the University of Tennessee at Chattanooga and with the city's arts and cultural institutions. Hamilton County has been recognized for its successful career academies, a program funded through public and private funds, which offer curricula related to particular industries such as construction and engineering. The county has 27 career academies in 14 high schools. In addition, Mayor Ron Littlefield instituted "The Great Ideas Competition" in 2005 to encourage student creativity in the areas of science, innovation, and entrepreneurship.

Private preparatory institutions such as the Girls Preparatory School, McCallie School, and Baylor School are nationally recognized for their numerous academic, athletic, enrichment, and community outreach programs. Chattanooga also has many faith-based elementary and secondary schools.

For higher education, Chattanooga offers a fine selection of excellent institutions for both academic and professional growth. The University of Tennessee at Chattanooga (UTC), long renowned for its nursing program, took a step toward becoming a leader in computational engineering with the opening in 2002 of its SimCenter for research and development. The center was made possible through both private and public funding. In November 2007, backed by $20 million in private funding, its name was changed to the SimCenter: National Center for Computational Engineering, reflecting its growing reputation in the field.

Like UTC, Southern Adventist University is a popular choice for those seeking a nursing career. Operated by the Seventh-day-Adventist Church, Southern Adventist University also offers programs in business and management, education, and computing, among others. Covenant College, with its spectacular location atop Lookout Mountain, is affiliated with the Presbyterian Church. With its focus on the liberal arts, Covenant offers associate's, bachelor's, and master's degrees, and also has several preprofessional programs. Other local, Christ-centered colleges include Lee University, with 48 undergraduate and graduate degrees; Bryan College, offering approximately 40 areas of study, including a nursing program in conjunction with Vanderbilt University; and Tennessee Temple University, with programs in 14 fields.

For those seeking vocational and/or technical training or in need of general-education classes for transfer, Chattanooga State Technical Community College provides a wide choice of programs, including engineering technology, business and information technologies, nursing, and liberal arts studies.

Outdoor Play

Chattanooga's natural surroundings of mountains, lakes, and rivers make it a destination for recreational activities of all kinds. With the region's mild weather, many of these activities may be enjoyed year-round.

For leisurely hikes, Chattanooga offers three greenways, linear parks reserved for public use. They are the South Chickamauga Creek Greenway, a 2.5-mile trail; the North Chickamauga Creek Greenway, which includes a canoe launch and a picnic area; and the 13-mile Tennessee Riverwalk, which winds from the Chickamauga Dam through many downtown parks and attractions.

This page, left: Black-eyed Susans on a hiking path at Rock City on Lookout Mountain. This page, right: Cumberland Caverns stalagmites. Opposite page: Rock City's Lover's Leap, with spectacular views from atop a 100-foot waterfall.

Those seeking more strenuous activities will never be at a loss. Rock climbers may test their skills at Sunset Rock or on Lookout Mountain, at the Tennessee Wall near Signal Mountain, or right in downtown Chattanooga at the Walnut Wall under the Walnut Street Bridge. Mountain bikers have a varied choice of terrain, from steep trails on Lookout and Signal mountains to gently sloping paths in Booker T. Washington State Park. With more than 7,000 caves within one hour's drive of the city, Chattanooga is a spelunker's dream, with caves rated for beginners through experienced cavers. Among these is Cumberland Caverns, Tennessee's largest show cave, approximately 60 miles from the city. In addition to these activities are opportunities for skiing, camping, skeet shooting, hunting, horseback riding, hang gliding, and sky diving.

Water lovers have many recreational opportunities along the Tennessee River Blueway, which runs from the Chickamauga Dam in Chattanooga through the beautiful Tennessee River Gorge to the Nickajack Dam in the neighboring county of Marion. Fishing, tubing, rowing, and even scuba diving as well as both flat-water and white-water rafting and paddling are just a few of the water activities available.

Throughout Chattanooga are scattered no fewer than 60 public parks with facilities for baseball, softball, football, basketball, golf, soccer, disc golf, in-line hockey, badminton, tennis, and much more. Some of the parks are situated on the riverfront. Among these are the recently opened Renaissance Park, a 23-acre wetlands in the heart of the city; Ross's Landing Park, home of the Tennessee Aquarium; and Coolidge Park, which features a restored, early 20th-century carousel.

Chattanooga also offers exciting spectator sports. The Chattanooga Lookouts, a Southern League Double A affiliate of baseball's Cincinnati Reds, play in downtown's 6,160-seat AT&T Field, which opened in 2000, replacing historic Engel Stadium as the home field. The team became a charter member of the Southern League in 1885. Former Lookouts players include National Baseball Hall of Fame members Burleigh Grimes, Ferguson Jenkins, and Harmon Killebrew.

Chattanooga is also home to the Chattanooga Locomotion of the National Women's Football Association (NWFA). As of 2007 the Chattanooga Locomotion was one of 32 NWFA teams across the country. The team is a three-time South Central Division champion.

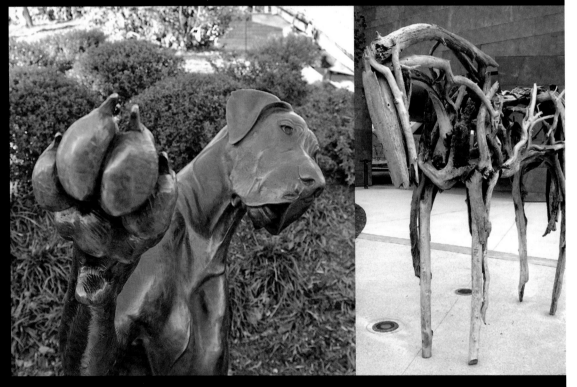

College football is a big part of the Chattanooga sports scene. The Mocs of the University of Tennessee at Chattanooga play at Finley Stadium Davenport Field. The venue is also the site of the NCAA Division I Football Championship, played every December.

For the Fun of It

Finley Stadium, which opened in 1997, was part of the Southside revitalization project, one of many such developments that contributed to the renaissance of downtown Chattanooga. The result is a city of stunning architecture, diverse arts and culture, and fascinating, fun attractions.

Defining the city's skyline is the Tennessee Aquarium, with its distinctive triangular glass rooftops and spectacular location overlooking the river. Opened in 1992, the aquarium was the first of the renaissance developments and has had a $1.5 billion economic impact on the city. Among the aquarium's 12,000 specimens are giant octopuses, otters, penguins, alligators, crocodiles, sharks, and red piranha. Also featured is an IMAX 3-D theater.

Children will enjoy the Creative Discovery Museum where they can explore RiverPlay, a climbing structure complete with a crow's nest, a spiral staircase, nets, and slides; exercise their talents in the artist's and musician's studios; dig for dinosaur bones and study rocks and minerals at the Excavation Station; or learn how things work at the Inventor's Clubhouse. Equally fascinating is the Chattanooga Zoo at Warner Park, six acres housing chimpanzees, red pandas, mountain lions, snow leopards, lemurs, and many other exotic creatures. Lake Winnepesaukah Amusement Park offers thrill rides and rides for the entire family or just for small children. The park features the nation's oldest mill chute ride, the Boat Chute, completed in 1927.

Chattanooga's rich history is celebrated at many sites throughout the area. Commemorating the beginning of the Trail of Tears is the Passage, part of the 21st Century Waterfront revitalization project downtown. The permanent outdoor exhibit features a wall embedded with seven ceramic disks which together tell the story of the Cherokee Nation. The history of Africans in Chattanooga is explored at the Chattanooga African American Museum, offering a look at some of the city's early black entrepreneurs. The city's railroad history is the topic at the Tennessee Valley Railroad Museum, where visitors may choose among several excursions aboard a vintage train. The Cincinnati Southern Railroad's locomotive, better known as the Chattanooga Choo Choo and inspiration for the song made famous by the Glenn Miller Orchestra, took its first journey in 1880, and into the 1940s passed through Chattanooga (as did nearly all the trains to the South then), stopping at Terminal Station. Today the station is the site of the Chattanooga Choo Choo Holiday Inn hotel and resort complex and is listed on the National Register of Historic Places.

Two blocks away via a glass pedestrian bridge is another architectural gem, the Hunter Museum of American Art. The museum showcases works of the Hudson River and Ashcan schools, American impressionists, abstract expressionists, and modern and contemporary artists. Located on the bluffs above the river, the museum consists of two buildings. The original, 1904 classical revival mansion contains 19th-century works, while 20th-century pieces are displayed in the contemporary building, opened in 1975. In 2004 an expansion added some 30,000 square feet of gallery space and won the museum an American Architecture Award from the Chicago Athenaeum, recognizing the most significant contemporary architectural projects in the United States.

Nearby is the historic Walnut Street Bridge. Built in 1890, it is the South's oldest truss bridge. Having served for nearly a century as a multipurpose bridge, it fell into disrepair but was rescued through a community effort and converted to a pedestrian bridge in 1993. Today it is one of the longest pedestrian bridges in the world.

Chattanooga's role in the Civil War can be explored at Chickamauga and Chattanooga National Military Park. The Battle of Chickamauga, fought in 1863, marked the last Confederate victory of the war. The first military park in the country, it opened in 1890 and includes Chickamauga and Lookout Mountain battlefields.

Lookout Mountain offers many additional attractions. Among these is Ruby Falls, with its spectacular 145-foot waterfall located in a cave 1,120 feet below ground. Additional geological formations are found in Rock City, as are a nature trail and panoramic views of seven states. The Incline Railway, billed as the world's steepest passenger railway, climbs to the top of the mountain on a track built at a 72.7 percent grade.

Opposite page, left: Historical buildings in the Bluff View Art District. Opposite page, right, and this page: Rembrandt's Coffee House in the Bluff View Art District.

On the Town

Day or night, Chattanooga offers a wealth of opportunities for shopping, dining, and entertainment.

The 1.1 million-square-foot Hamilton Place complex, one of the largest shopping centers in the Southeast, consists of Hamilton Place, Hamilton Crossing, Hamilton Corner, the Terrace, and the Shoppes. Together these venues feature more than 200 stores, including Dillard's, Belk, JCPenney, Sears, Ann Taylor, and Banana Republic; 17 movie screens; and 30 eateries. Hamilton Place attracts more than 16 million shoppers each year. Northgate Mall is anchored by JCPenney, Belk, Sears, and T. J. Maxx and features an additional 100-plus specialty stores, 10 eateries, and a 14-screen cinema. Other favorite venues include Frazier Avenue, with its unique restaurants and boutiques, and the Bluff View Art District, with its many studios and galleries, restaurants, and coffee shops.

The historic Tivoli Theatre is home to the Chattanooga Symphony and Opera. The company produces four series each year: the Masterworks, Opera, Pops, and Chamber series. The venue also presents Broadway and children's shows, comedians, and musical artists such as Emmylou Harris, Shawn Colvin, B. B. King, George Jones, the Temptations, and the Four Tops. The Bessie Smith Hall, named for the great blues singer and Chattanooga native, is a 264-seat hall for concerts, lectures, and workshops and is also ideal for conventions and meetings.

Chattanoogans love a festival, and with its riverfront venues and mild weather year-round, downtown Chattanooga is the perfect place to throw a community-wide party. One of the largest and most popular festivals is Riverbend, which every June hosts more than 100 artists on six stages over nine evenings. The festival began in 1981 and attracts more than 650,000 people. Artists showcased in 2007 included Vince Gill; Ricky Scaggs; the Steve Miller Band; and Earth, Wind, and Fire. Nightfall, which celebrates its 20th season in 2008, is a summerlong event featuring an international array of performers. Late November brings Winter Days and Lights, a three-week series of holiday-themed events, from the Grand Illumination on the River to a parade and holiday concert. During the festival, more than 130 downtown buildings are adorned with sparkling lights.

Chattanooga is also home to Go!Fest, founded in 2005 by Mayor Ron Littlefield to celebrate the goals and talents of people with disabilities. The festival promotes their inclusion in city life by showing them the many facilities and opportunities that exist in Chattanooga to help them realize their personal and career goals.

Chattanooga in the past 200 years has truly carved out its place in history and become a place where anyone and everyone is welcome to call the Scenic City of the South home.

CHAPTER TWO

MADE IN CHATTANOOGA

Manufacturing and Food Processing

Chattanooga's manufacturing sector employs some 34,000 people and makes up more than 15 percent of the city's economy. According to the Chattanooga Manufacturers Association, employees in Chattanooga's manufacturing sector earn on average 18 percent more than their counterparts nationally. The city offers an extensive rail network; easy access to river ports; and one-day trucking to virtually 75 percent of the United States via three interstates. Chattanooga is no less than a five-star community in terms of logistics. It is also home to Enterprise South, a leading industrial park in the Southeast.

From the sweetest snacks to the most durable construction products, from chemicals to appliances, Chattanooga's manufacturing output is an eclectic mix. In fact, *Southern Business and Development* magazine featured the city in its spring 2006 issue as one of the top 10 southern midmarkets with highly diverse economies.

In Good Taste

Some of the nation's favorite foods are made right here in Chattanooga. Everyone recognizes the box featuring a curly-headed youngster in a cowgirl hat. Little Debbie snack cakes are made by one of Chattanooga's largest employers, McKee Foods. The family-run company, which got its start not long after founder O. D. McKee began selling five-cent snack cakes from the back of his car in the 1930s, now provides jobs for some 3,200 area workers. The original bakery was established with three employees and a recipe for oatmeal cream pies. Today McKee Foods produces more than 100 varieties of snack cakes—making Little Debbie one of the nation's leading snack cake brands—and posts annual sales in excess of $1 billion. And the little girl on the packaging? That would be McKee's granddaughter, complete with a crease in the brim of her hat where she once sat on it.

This page: Enjoying a MoonPie in a 1950s Chattanooga market.
Opposite page: Pilgrim's Pride poultry processing plant.

Arguably the most recognized logo in the world is that of Coca-Cola, and Chattanooga played an important role in that company's history as home to its first bottling plant, opened in 1899. The plant, originally at 17 Market Street, was a factor in turning the drink into a national—and then international—sensation and led to the establishment of other such plants, thus increasing the product's distribution. Today the company operates as a franchise under the name Chattanooga Coca-Cola Bottling Company.

Another favorite beverage company, Double-Cola was founded in Chattanooga in 1922 as the Good Grape Company, to sell grape soda. The business gained fame in 1933 when it introduced its sodas in 12-ounce bottles, twice the standard soda bottle size. Today the company is owned by the British firm K. J. International but maintains its roots in Chattanooga, with its corporate headquarters located downtown. Double-Cola Co.–USA makes Double-Cola, Ski, and Jumbo beverages, among other popular products.

That popular southern treat, the MoonPie, also got its start in Chattanooga. Its maker, the Chattanooga Bakery, was founded at the turn of the 20th century as a subsidiary of the Mountain City Flour Mill. As company lore would have it, a salesman asked coal miners in his territory what they might like for a snack.

They requested something solid and filling, and when the salesman asked what size it should be, one of the workers raised his hands to frame the rising moon and said, "About that big!" The marshmallow, chocolate, and graham cracker confection was famously paired with RC Cola back in the 1950s. Today, in addition to MoonPies, Chattanooga Bakery manufactures "double decker" and minivarieties in four flavors. The privately held company employs some 150 people and had 2007 sales of nearly $14 million.

Wm. Wrigley Jr. Company chose Chattanooga as the site for the production of its Altoid brand mints. In 2005 the company acquired a former Kraft Foods facility, investing $23 million in its expansion, adding not only 60,000 square feet of space but 150 full-time jobs.

Pilgrim's Pride—which produces chicken, turkey, eggs, deli, and salad items—is Chattanooga's fourth-largest employer. Based in Pittsburg, Texas, the company employs around 2,000 people at its Chattanooga facility, where it makes cooked chicken products and processes poultry, fish, and meat products.

Chemicals, Carpets, and Construction

Chattanooga's diverse manufacturing roster includes chemicals and pharmaceuticals. Chattem produces a long and varied list of over-the-counter drugs and other products sold in this country and in Canada, South and Central America, Europe, and the Caribbean. Among these are Gold Bond powder, Icy Hot pain reliever, Bullfrog sunscreen, Mudd facial masks, Aspercreme topical analgesic, Pamprin for menstrual symptoms, Benzodent oral analgesic, and Melatonex sleep aid. In addition, in 2006, Chattem picked up Balmex, Kaopectate, Cortizone, Act, and Unisom from Johnson & Johnson. The company has been around since 1879, operating first under the name the Chattanooga Medicine Company. Today it employs 350 people and posts annual sales of around $300 million.

Chattanooga's proximity to the carpet-industry center of Dalton, Georgia, means that textiles, polymers, and other products related to that industry make up a large part of Chattanooga's manufacturing base.

Several manufacturers of polymers are headquartered or have a presence in the Chattanooga area. Alco Chemical was founded in Philadelphia in 1927; but 35 years later the company moved its manufacturing operations to Chattanooga to better support Dalton's booming carpet industry. As a center for the manufacture of carpet, textile, and upholstery compounds, Chattanooga offered a good fit—so much so that in 1980 the company moved the rest of its operations here. Alco was acquired by National Starch and Chemical Company in 1989, and National Starch was acquired by ICI in 1997. Alco remains a worldwide supplier of aqueous and emulsion polymers as well as sulfonated and carbon disulfide products.

Opposite page, left and center: Alco's Chattanooga facility. This page: Employee of BASF, which has two facilities in Chattanooga.

Another important Chattanooga employer is Propex, the leading maker of fibers and fabrics for furnishings, geosynthetics, concrete reinforcement, and more. Each year, its products are used in roughly half of the carpeting made throughout the world. Its brand names include Fibermesh, Duon, Actionbac, Pyramat, and ArmorMax, to name but a few. In addition to its headquarters, Propex also has manufacturing facilities in Chattanooga. There are five additional U.S. plants, all located in Georgia, as well as sales offices, plants, distribution centers, and technical support offices in Mexico, Brazil, Germany, Hungary, and the United Kingdom.

Shaw Industries, based in Dalton, Georgia, makes both carpet and flooring. Shaw employs roughly 1,000 employees in the Chattanooga area. It began back in 1946 as the Star Dye Company, which dyed tufted scatter rugs. Shaw was the first floor covering manufacturer to be named a "top 100 training company" by *Training* magazine, joining other noteworthy organizations like IBM and Microsoft.

A manufacturer of performance and textile fibers with operations in Chattanooga is INVISTA, which is owned by Koch Industries of Wichita, Kansas. The company's brand names include Lycra, Stainmaster, and Thermolite. Its Chattanooga facility supports a 200-acre preserve that was the National Institute for Urban Wildlife's first such certified conservation area in Tennessee. The preserve was also certified "highest habitat" by the Wildlife Habitat Enhancement Council.

Astec Industries, with close to 1,100 workers, is among the top-10 largest employers in the area. Astec is the country's leading manufacturer of equipment for asphalt-road building, pipeline and utility trenching, and aggregate processing. Founded in 1972 and headquartered in Chattanooga, Astec manufactures in excess of 170 products and occupies more than 440,000 square feet of office and manufacturing space in the city.

Chattanooga is headquarters for Heil Environmental, which makes state-of-the-art refuse- and recycling-collection vehicles. Its chief manufacturing facility is located in nearby Fort Payne, Alabama. The company also has plants in Greenville, South Carolina, and in Hillend, Scotland, and employs approximately 1,000 people worldwide. A subsidiary of Dover Corporation of New York, Heil owns more than 200 U.S. patents.

Chattanooga is home to two manufacturing plants of Germany-based chemical company BASF. Produced here are styrene-butadiene polymer dispersions for use as carpet backing, foams, paper coating, asphalt modifiers, and adhesives. BASF employs approximately 130 people at its Chattanooga facilities.

Traditional and heavy manufacturing also play important roles in the local economy. Siskin Steel & Supply Company, headquartered in Chattanooga, distributes aluminum and steel products throughout the Southeast. It began in 1900 as a scrap-metal business and has gone on to develop metal service centers in Chattanooga and Nashville; as well in Birmingham, Alabama; and Spartanburg, South Carolina.

Chattanooga was the birthplace of the tow truck, and Miller Industries, based in nearby Ooltewah, carries on that tradition by producing car carriers, light- and heavy-duty wreckers, and multivehicle trailers as well as parts and accessories. In 2006 it modernized its Chattanooga plant, adding 50,000 square feet of floor space and upgraded equipment.

Further illustrating Chattanooga's diverse manufacturing sector are Top Flight, a family-run, 80-year-old manufacturer and distributor of paper-based products such as notebooks and envelopes; PlayCore, a leader in park, playground, and fitness equipment that has been around since the 1920s; and Roper Home Appliances, a division of Whirlpool Corporation in Lafayette, Georgia, that makes washers, dryers, dishwashers, ranges, and refrigerators. Hamilton Plastics, a producer of lamination films and plastic bags for food packaging, celebrated 20 years in Chattanooga in 2006 with a 160,000-square-foot expansion and 25 new jobs. Offering custom-manufacturing and precision-engineering services to the hydroelectric, nuclear, and power industries is East Tech Company. Established in Chattanooga in 2004, East Tech has grown so quickly that in 2007 it built a new, 30,000-square-foot headquarters facility, tripling its original space. Founded in 1990, Sofix is the national leader in the manufacture of color formers, chemical powders used to create images on barcode labels, receipts, tickets and other carbonless- or thermal-paper products.

Manufacturers in Chattanooga benefit from the work of the Chattanooga Manufacturers Association in such areas as public policy, energy costs, employee training, utility rates, environmental standards, and more. Established in the city in 1902, the association counts approximately 250 Chattanooga manufacturers among its members.

Chattanooga indeed offers many advantages to manufacturers and food processors, from its reasonable utility rates to excellent infrastructure, from its strategic location to its educated and skilled workforce.

CHAPTER THREE

MIND AND BODY
Education and Health Care

Education and health care—two primary concerns of Americans today—are products both of long-standing traditions of excellence and innovative technological advances. Chattanooga's universities and hospitals, some of which have served the community for 100 years or more, are working to adapt their historic institutions to the new demands—and opportunities—of the 21st century.

A New Synergy

In Chattanooga, a new synergy was discovered between the private and public education sectors, which joined forces to create a vital new higher educational institution—the University of Tennessee at Chattanooga (UTC). Chattanooga University, founded as a private college in 1886, merged with the University of Tennessee, one of the nation's oldest land-grant universities, in 1969. The original downtown campus covers 120 acres; an additional 200 acres at Enterprise South, the former Volunteer Army Ammunitions Plant, was ceded to the university by the federal government, providing a site for biological research and future expansion. More than 91 percent of the 7,544 undergraduate students hail from Hamilton County and other counties in the Volunteer State. They can select from 43 majors and 39 minors.

Students going on to pursue graduate studies can choose from 21 programs, including computational engineering. Established in 2002, this program has more than 20 full-time faculty and staff, whose teaching, research, and career experience are invaluable assets. The UTC SimCenter, a 31,000-square-foot research and education facility that opened in 2003, partners with industry and government entities to develop analytical and design tools for real-world engineering problems. With a $3.5 million appropriation from the U.S. Senate, the center was green-lighted to house and test a 100-kilowatt fuel cell. Clean, efficient, the fuel cell could prove to be an important new source of energy.

Universities with religious affiliations and a faith-based approach to academics and student life are found in almost biblical abundance in Chattanooga. Southern Adventist University, founded in a room over a general store in 1892, is operated by the Seventh-day Adventist Church. In 1996, the university changed its name from Southern College of Seventh-day Adventists to Southern Adventist University, reflecting its new status as a university; that same year, the first graduate classes were held. The student body of approximately 2,500 students, most of whom belong to the Adventist denomination, can choose from among more than 70 undergraduate degrees. Nearly a quarter of the students attend the School of Nursing, which boasts a nearly 100 percent passing rate on the licensure exam on the first attempt. In addition to nursing, graduate degrees are also offered in business, computing, education, psychology and, of course, religion.

Culturally, Southern Adventist stays in tune with its School of Music, whose musical offerings include a symphony orchestra, a wind symphony, a jazz ensemble, and several choral groups. Under the tutelage of Professor Judy Glass, organ students can pull out all the stops on the 70-stop Brombaugh tracker organ; three were proficient enough to earn Fulbright Scholarships. Not to be outdone, the School of Visual Art and Design created a feature film, *Secret of the Cave*, that won a Crystal Heart Award at the 2006 Heartland Film Festival and was screened at the 2007 Santa Barbara Film Festival. The Lynn H. Wood Archaeological Museum houses a collection of more than 300 sherds from throughout the Near East, as well as an ancient brick from the city of Babylon and bearing Nebuchadnezzar's seal.

The 1,000-acre campus in Collegedale, seven miles from Chattanooga, also affords rich and varied recreational opportunities. Students can enjoy miles of hiking trails, a natural rock-climbing wall, and a ropes course. They can also avail themselves of the state-of-the-art Hulsey Wellness Center, with its heated pool, rock-climbing wall, and workout equipment. Fit in mind and body, students are also encouraged to maintain spiritual fitness by participating in ministries and outreach programs.

Nestled in the foothills of the Appalachian Mountains in Cleveland, Tennessee, Lee University was founded in 1918 and today is the Volunteer State's largest Christ-centered private institution. In a two-decade period, the enrollment more than tripled, to 4,000-plus students in 2006. In 1997 Lee College became Lee University; Lee attained new status as a "Masters University" in the *U.S. News & World Report* college rankings for 2008. This new stature reflects the growing enrollment, increased diversity of its undergraduate programs, and the expanded graduate programs. That Lee embraces science as well as religion was underscored in 2007, when the Department of Natural Sciences and Mathematics was awarded a Genomics Education Matching Fund from LI-COR, a bioscience research company, that financed the purchase of a 4300 DNA Analysis System. This state-of-the-art system, among the most important tools in molecular biology, allows researchers to identify every base in a section of DNA.

A "castle in the clouds" is the setting for Covenant College, Founded in 1955 in Pasadena, California, the college moved to St. Louis, then in 1964 took up residence in the former Lookout Mountain Hotel in Lookout Mountain, Georgia, just across the border from Tennessee and only minutes from Chattanooga. Ranked seventh in the *U.S. News & World Report*'s 2008 rankings for baccalaureate colleges in the South, this small, liberal arts college also earned a spot on MSNBC's "Pretty College Campuses" list for its 300-acre mountaintop setting. Of more than 1,250 students from 47 states and 17 countries, more than 900 are undergraduates, all of whom are professing Christians, a requirement for admission. With a 14-to-one student-faculty ratio, undergraduate programs include education; computer science and information systems; and pre-med, nursing, engineering, and ministerial programs. Anticipating growth in its programs and student body, the college embarked on a $31 million initiative, BUILD, to add new facilities, renovate existing ones, and expand the already lavish green spaces.

Providing students with marketable technical skills is the goal of Chattanooga State Technical Community College. Founded in 1965 as Chattanooga State Technical Institute, the school moved to its present location on the Tennessee River in 1967 and changed its name in 1973, merging with the State Area Vocational-Technical School in 1981. Today, with more than 8,000 students in attendance, the college offers one- and two-year programs in a variety of health-related fields, including nursing, physical therapy, dental hygiene, and radiology. Students can also learn everything from computer operations to air-conditioning and auto repair.

A graduate program in Christian counseling is offered by the Psychological Studies Institute (PSI), with campuses in Chattanooga and Atlanta. The result of a merger of the Chattanooga Bible Institute and Atlanta Clinical College in 2000, PSI offers a master of arts in professional counseling and in marriage and family therapy, along with a master of science in Christian psychological studies. PSI integrates Christian faith and psychological principles through a curriculum of biblical studies, applied theology, and practical theology. PSI also offers practical experience through a network of counseling centers staffed by students, faculty, and alumni.

In Good Health

In 1889 Baron Frederic Emile d'Erlanger, a French nobleman, donated $5,000 for a new hospital in downtown Chattanooga. Named for his wife, Baroness Marguerite Mathilde Slidell, the hospital opened in 1891, thus laying the cornerstone for health care in the Chattanooga area. Nearly a century later, Erlanger has five campuses offering a comprehensive array of medical services for children and adults.

Children suffering from illness or injury receive treatment at T. C. Thompson Children's Hospital, a Comprehensive Regional Pediatric Center (CRPC) located on the downtown campus. The Level III neonatal intensive care unit provides highly skilled, around-the-clock care for premature babies and newborns with medical conditions. Cardiology, cardiovascular surgery, treatment of cancer and blood disorders, along with psychology and physical therapy, are among the broad array of pediatric specialties provided at Thompson.

In 1989, nearly a century after the hospital's founding, the area's first kidney transplant was performed at the Erlanger Kidney Transplant Center. Over the ensuing two decades, the center has performed nearly 500 transplants, providing a full continuum of care for its patients. In 2005, the surgeons at Erlanger began performing laparoscopic living donor nephrectomies, which helps minimize postoperative pain and allows for a quicker recovery time. Erlanger helps to match patients with donor organs quickly and efficiently, and a multidisciplinary team of kidney specialists, surgeons, nurses, dieticians, and social counselors works closely with the patients to determine their specific needs.

People suffering from life-threatening trauma are transported to Erlanger's emergency care facility by the Life Force air ambulance program, which is equipped with two Bell 412 helicopters and one Bell 206L4 helicopter, along with ground ambulances. Once admitted, patients receive the needed care provided by Erlanger's broad array of specialties. In addition to the region's first accredited chest pain center and wound care center, Erlanger operates the area's only emergency heart and stroke center. Cancer patients receive state-of-the-art treatment at the Erlanger Cancer Center, which operates a clinical research program and a resource center for patients. The Miller Eye Center, located on the Baroness Campus, houses the Lion's Eye Bank, one in a worldwide network of eye banks sponsored by the Lion's Club. The Tennessee Craniofacial Center is a leader in facial reconstruction. The Sleep Disorders Center at the Erlanger North Campus helps the growing number of people with chronic sleep problems. The Chattanooga LifeStyle Center offers a variety of fitness, rehabilitation, and education programs. The physical and emotional issues of aging are addressed through the senior's program, an in-patient service on the North Campus.

Opposite page: Reception area at Memorial Hospital's new MaryEllen Locher Breast Center. This page: Oncological surgeons at work at Memorial Hospital.

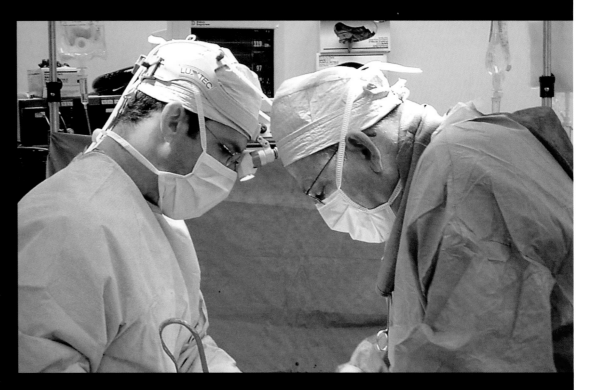

One of the region's leading teaching hospitals, Erlanger is home of the University of Tennessee College of Medicine–Chattanooga Unit, which offers training for medical students, along with eight residency programs and fellowships in surgical critical care and geriatric medicine.

Memorial Health Care System is one of the leading health care providers in the Southeast. Its two acute-care hospitals—Memorial Hospital and Memorial North Park Hospital—are complemented by more than 700 physicians in 30 locations and by home health care services. The community-based Cancer Care Program offers a multidisciplinary approach to the treatment of cancer, which includes screening and early diagnosis and state-of-the-art technology. Clinical trials for breast cancer, pancreatic cancer, and melanoma are conducted in conjunction with the Eastern Cooperative Oncology Group (ECOG) and the Vanderbilt-Ingram Cancer Center Affiliate Network (VICCAN), as well as with pharmaceutical companies. Dedicated to caring for the mind and spirit as well as the body, Memorial provides services that include massage therapy, Reiki therapy, creative movement, art therapy, and other programs to help reduce stress and improve the quality of life for cancer patients and their families. In February 2007 Memorial celebrated the opening of the state-of-the-art MaryEllen Locher Breast Center.

When a patient suffering chest pain is wheeled into Memorial's emergency room, the "Chest Pain Protocol" is immediately put into effect to ensure prompt diagnosis and treatment of a potentially life-threatening condition. Memorial's Regional Heart Center performs more than 700 open-heart surgeries each year, double those performed at any other area hospital. Both Memorial and North Park have Chest Pain Centers that use advanced technology for the diagnosis and treatment of cardiac illness.

Using sophisticated procedures and a team approach, the orthopedic specialists at Memorial's Joint Replacement Center provide total knee and hip replacements. Using digital X-ray imaging, high-technology fiber optics, and MRI, orthopedic surgeons also perform hundreds of arthroscopic surgeries each year to repair shoulders, knees, elbows, wrists, and ankles.

Built entirely with capital from private investors, Parkridge Medical Center opened in 1971 and in 2000 began a $36 million expansion that included the Sarah Cannon Cancer Center. The facility was named for Sarah Cannon, the creator of the beloved character Minnie Pearl, who herself battled cancer. Affiliated with a network of 400 participating oncologists in 22 states, the center offers a number of specialties—hematology, gynecologic oncology, urology, cardiology, and more. Knowing that early detection is critical in fighting cancer, the staff is committed to seeing patients within 24 hours. Parkridge Medical Center also offers a full range of cardiac services, and on staff are surgeons who specialize in the da Vinci Surgical System, which allows them to perform minimally invasive procedures using robotic technology.

Since it opened in downtown Chattanooga in 1990, the Siskin Hospital for Physical Rehabilitation has offered specialized treatment programs for brain injuries, spinal cord injuries, strokes, amputations, orthopedics, and major multiple trauma. Built with wide hallways, large patient rooms and bathrooms, and inviting common areas, the facility provides a full continuum of care from the onset of the patient's illness or injury until his or her return to home, work, or school.

Chattanooga's medical facilities, along with its institutions of higher education, are meeting the enormous challenges inherent in providing quality, state-of-the-art education and health care for children and adults. Ensuring that young people, regardless of socioeconomic status, have an opportunity to attend college and that citizens of all ages and economic backgrounds have access to needed medical services are daunting tasks. However, innovative new approaches such as the UT SimCenter and the Sarah Cannon Cancer Center have proven that Chattanooga has the capability to provide its citizens with quality education and health care.

CHAPTER FOUR

A FOUNDATION FOR SUCCESS

Professional and Consumer Services

For any economy to grow and prosper, it must have a solid foundation of professional services. Chattanooga's banks, insurance companies, accountants, law firms, and other professionals offer a well-established, reputable, and comprehensive network of services to businesses already established in or planning a move to Chattanooga.

Consider that, as of June 2006, the area's banks and thrifts were reporting total deposits of $1.1 billion. Consider, too, that Chattanooga is home to both BlueCross BlueShield of Tennessee and Unum, two of the biggest names in the insurance sector, to nationally recognized accounting and law firms, and to major players in real estate and facility management. With this diverse core of professional and consumer services, Chattanooga offers businesses a launching pad for success.

This page, left: Growing funds with an account in a Chattanooga bank. This page, right: Cornerstone Community Bank's downtown Chattanooga offices, on Georgia Avenue. Opposite page: The convenience of online banking.

Dollars and Sense

Chattanooga's financial services providers are many and varied, from community banks to international megacorporations.

Cornerstone Community Bank, for example, opened its first branch in Chattanooga in 1996. Today, the Chattanooga-based company has locations in southeast Tennessee and in north Georgia and counts more than 5,000 businesses among its clients. In fact, the bank caters to businesses, which make up 80 percent of its client base. Cornerstone offers boutique banking, including nontraditional services such as remote deposit and asset-based lending, and is one of the largest small business administration lenders in the state. So far, Community's strategy has proved successful; the bank was ranked among the top 100 banks in the country in a 2007 survey of more than 8,100 peer banks by *U.S. Banker* magazine. As of June 2006, Cornerstone had more than $338 million in assets.

Like Cornerstone, First Security Group, which operates as FSGBank, runs locally owned and operated institutions. FSGBank caters primarily to individuals who live in communities along the interstates of East and Middle Tennessee and North Georgia. It operates six branches in Chattanooga. The company has 38 full-service banking offices operating under the names FSGBank, Jackson Bank & Trust, Dalton Whitfield Bank, and Primer Banco Seguro. The organization's sales for 2006, up almost 32 percent from the year prior, were close to $86 million.

Opposite page: First Volunteer Bank's Broad Street office. This page, left: The main Chattanooga office of SunTrust Bank, on Market Street. This page, right: Expert and efficient service offered by Chattanooga bankers.

Other Chattanooga-based financial institutions include First Volunteer Bank of Tennessee and the Tennessee Valley Federal Credit Union. First Volunteer Bank of Tennessee started out as Marion Trust and Banking in 1904 and is today a 21-branch organization spread across East and Middle Tennessee. Originally headquartered in Jasper, the multimarket company moved its corporate offices to Chattanooga in 2001. First Volunteer posts annual sales of nearly $37 million. The company also offers insurance through its First Volunteer Insurance agencies, located in two of the company's bank branches in Chattanooga and in one in Jasper.

With more than $21 million in annual sales, the Tennessee Valley Federal Credit Union offers loan, credit card, and banking services to its nearly 73,000 members. These members are from more than 1,200 employee groups in the Tennessee Valley. The company has 12 full-service branches and employs more than 100 people in the greater Chattanooga area.

Three of the South's largest banks have a major presence in Chattanooga. Among these is Atlanta-based SunTrust Banks, one of the country's largest financial holding companies, with assets of more than $180 billion. With 33 branches within 50 miles of Chattanooga, including many located in Wal-Mart stores, SunTrust has more than 22 percent of the Chattanooga area market share in terms of deposits.

First Horizon National Corporation, which operates as both First Tennessee Bank and First Horizon Bank, is the largest bank in the state and one of the largest in Chattanooga in deposit market share. Headquartered in Memphis, the company has 15 First Tennessee branches within a 10-mile radius of Chattanooga's center. Overall there are 230 First Tennessee and First Horizon banks in Tennessee, Arkansas, Georgia, Mississippi, and Virginia. First Horizon offers services in retail and commercial banking, mortgage banking, and capital markets as well as health savings accounts, venture capital, equipment financing, and more. It has been named one of the 100 Best Corporate Citizens by *Business Ethics* magazine; is on the AARP's list of the Best Employers for Workers over 50; made *Fortune* magazine's Hall of Fame as a top company to work for; and for more than a decade has consistently been rated among *Working Mother* magazine's 100 Best Companies for Working Mothers.

With more than 20 percent of the city's deposit market share is Regions Bank, part of Regions Financial Corporation, based in Birmingham, Alabama. A 2006 merger between Regions and AmSouth Bankcorporation brought the company's assets to nearly $140 billion, with nearly $100 billion in deposits, making Regions Financial Corporation among the 10 largest bank holding companies in the United States. The 16-state organization has approximately 2,000 branches, with more than 20 of these in the Chattanooga area.

Chattanooga's banking community continues to grow as does Chattanooga's reputation as a strong center for business. In March 2007 CapitalMark Bank & Trust was founded in Chattanooga. The company already boasts more than $109 million in assets and in late 2007 opened its second office, in Knoxville. FirstBank, based in Lexington, Tennessee, announced in January 2008 that it planned to open two branches in Chattanooga in the spring. With $1.9 billion in assets, FirstBank is the largest independently owned bank in the state.

Confidence Builder

The insurance industry is also a major contributor to Chattanooga's economy, with some of the nation's largest insurers headquartered or having branch offices here.

Unum, the largest disability and long-term-care insurer in the United States, has some 10,000 employees worldwide, 3,000 of them in the Chattanooga area, where the company has been headquartered since its founding in 1887. The Fortune 250 company, which changed its name from UnumProvident in 2007, serves approximately 21 million employees of more than 100,000 companies. In addition to its disability and long-term-care coverage, Unum is a provider of group life and voluntary workplace benefits. The company, which is also the leading employee benefits provider in the United Kingdom, recorded sales of more than $10.5 billion in 2006. In addition to its Chattanooga headquarters, Unum has offices in California, Maine, Massachusetts, and South Carolina.

Also a major employer in Chattanooga is CIGNA Healthcare of Tennessee. Though CIGNA HealthCare is based in Bloomfield, Connecticut, the company employs more than 800 Chattanoogans in its downtown offices and serves some 1.3 million members nationwide. CIGNA provides medical-benefits plans, dental coverage, pharmacy benefits, behavioral health coverage, and more. The company's net income at the end of 2006 was $1.2 billion.

Expert Advice

Businesses in and around Chattanooga recognize that experience is essential when it comes to financial planning and legal matters.

Chattanooga is home to many well-established accounting firms offering expertise in a variety of areas. Among these is Hazlett, Lewis & Bieter, better known as HLB. The firm, which began in 1943, employs 60 people and specializes in accounting, business consulting, and auditing. HLB serves local clients as well as clients in Nashville, Knoxville, Memphis, and Atlanta. The industries represented include financial institutions, government, health care, manufacturing, construction, and nonprofits.

BlueCross BlueShield of Tennessee (BCBST) was founded in 1945 and today is the largest not-for-profit managed care provider in the state. BCBST offers plans for both groups and individuals and also offers Medicaid and Medicare plans and coverage in a wide variety of areas including disability, life, vision and dental, and long-term care, among others. With annual sales of $3 billion, BCBST has 13 subsidiaries and affiliates in Tennessee and across the country. The Chattanooga-based, locally governed company has more than 4,000 local employees, and more than two million Tennesseans are covered by BCBST health plans, and more than five million benefit from BlueCross BlueShield services nationwide. The company is building a new downtown headquarters campus, expected to open in 2009.

Joseph Decosimo and Company boasts the largest number of certified public accountants of any accounting firm based in Tennessee. With more than 250 professionals and staff on its roster, the company was ranked as one of the country's top-10 fastest-growing accounting firms in 2006. Founded in 1971, the company serves a long list of industries, including health care, manufacturing and distribution, financial institutions, construction, and more. Areas of expertise include corporate finance, litigation support, assurance, and international and domestic tax concerns. In addition to its Chattanooga office, Joseph Decosimo and Company has locations in Knoxville, Memphis, and Nashville, Tennessee; in Atlanta and Dalton, Georgia; in Cincinnati, Ohio; and in the Cayman Islands.

Chattanooga's well-established law firms include Miller & Martin, founded in 1867. It is a full-service firm with offices in Chattanooga, Nashville, and Atlanta. The downtown Chattanooga location serves as the firm's main office. Miller & Martin employs more than 180 attorneys—nearly 100 of them in Chattanooga. The firm's nearly 40 areas of practice include international, intellectual property, securities, entertainment, labor and employment, health care, and technology and licensing law as well as tax matters. The company is also one of 46 members of the noted World Law Group (WLG), an international network of more than 10,000 lawyers. Membership in the WLG is by invitation only.

Husch & Eppenberger was the first national law firm to establish a presence in the Chattanooga area. Headquartered in St. Louis, the company has two Chattanooga locations where approximately 36 lawyers practice in such areas as labor and employment, health care, insurance coverage, intellectual property, antitrust, class actions, commercial, environmental, construction, products liability, and toxic torts.

Serving with Distinction

Other professional service providers based in Chattanooga include CBL & Associates Properties. Founded in 1978, the company is a leading mall real estate investment trust and has either an interest in or manages approximately 130 properties in 26 states. Among these is Hamilton Place, located in Chattanooga and the largest regional mall in Tennessee. CBL expanded to China in 2006 and plans to increase its international footprint over the next few years.

Serving shopping malls, airports, food-processing companies, commercial construction firms, and businesses in other fields is ERMC. With a national presence, ERMC offers airline and airport services, janitorial and housekeeping services, construction and construction clean-up, facility maintenance, security and patrol services, facilities business management consulting services, and much more. Founded in 1972, ERMC employs more than 4,000 people and averages $89 million in annual sales.

The Chattanooga business community benefits from these and many other professional-service providers, as do many companies across the nation and around the world. This fast-growing sector will continue to provide entrepreneurs with a foundation for success.

CHAPTER FIVE

MAKING CONNECTIONS

Transportation, Energy, and Telecommunications

The train celebrated in the Glenn Miller ode "Chattanooga Choo-Choo" exists no longer—indeed, much has changed in the past hundred years in transportation, energy, and telecommunications. Air travel, nuclear power, and the Internet were undreamed of when "Chattanooga Choo-Choo" was a hit song, but today these are among the cornerstones of a city merging into the fast lane of the 21st century.

A Moving Experience

Visitors to downtown Chattanooga can ride the Downtown Electric Shuttle, which runs daily from the Chattanooga Choo Choo (now a hotel and convention complex) to the Tennessee Aquarium, with convenient downtown access to the convention center, shopping, and hotels. Operated by the Chattanooga Area Regional Transportation Authority (CARTA), the quiet, environmentally friendly fleet of shuttles has logged more than 11.3 million passenger trips since it started service in 1992. CARTA's 16 bus routes offer unlimited rides for a modest $40 per month. CARTA also operates the Lookout Mountain Incline Railway, the world's steepest passenger railway, and Care-A-Van, a curb-to-curb service for disabled passengers.

This page: The Downtown Electric Shuttle. Opposite page: Chattanooga Metropolitan Airport.

Chattanooga has spread its wings with flights to thousands of worldwide destinations from the Chattanooga Metropolitan Airport. Carriers serving the airport include American Eagle, Continental Express, Delta Connection, Northwest Airlink, U.S. Airways Express, and Allegiant Air. They offer nonstop service to Atlanta, Charlotte, Cincinnati, Chicago, Memphis, Houston, Dallas, ,and Washington, D.C. In 2006, nonstop flights to Tampa/St. Petersburg and Orlando were added through Allegiant Air. Increased competition among carriers has led to decreased fares—this, along with the convenience of a smaller regional airport, helped to generate a 19 percent increase in passenger boardings in the first quarter of 2007 as compared to the same period in 2006.

More than 40 percent of outbound air travelers from the Chattanooga area go through Hartsfield-Jackson Atlanta International Airport, the world's busiest airport in number of passengers. Through this and other nearby major hubs, passengers can book connecting flights to domestic cities, from New York to Los Angeles and worldwide destinations, from London to Tokyo to Beijing.

To increase passenger traffic through the airport by a minimum of 10 percent, or at least 500,000 passengers, by 2008, the Chattanooga Metropolitan Airport Authority implemented a strategic plan, the cornerstone of which is building reliable, convenient service and offering consistently competitive fares. Plans are under way to provide service to Chattanooga's number-one leisure destination, Las Vegas, and to continue nonstop service to New York's LaGuardia Airport.

The transport of goods and services to destinations throughout North America calls for an efficient fleet of trucks. In 1986, Max Fuller and Patrick Quinn bought a number of transportation-related companies and merged them into U.S. Xpress. Today the Chattanooga-based company operates a fleet of 7,500 tractors and 20,500 trailers that provide medium- and long-haul service across the country, as well as regional service to cities in the Midwest, Southeast, and West. Truck transportation accounts for more than 90 percent of the company's overall sales. Xpress Global Systems, a subsidiary, provides less-than-truckload freight hauling, warehousing, and distribution to clients in the floor-covering industry.

One of the first carriers to use satellite communications, U.S. Xpress employs a sophisticated e-business platform to increase productivity and provide on-time delivery for its customers, which include retailers, manufacturers, and other transportation companies. Employing more than 8,000 professionals, the company earned its third Quest for Quality Award from *Logistics Management & Distribution Magazine,* in 2007.

To remain competitive, the company offers such innovative services as "near airfreight," using a team of drivers on long-haul routes to provide fast delivery at a lower cost than air freight. The company also contracts with railroads to deliver freight via high-speed rail rather than by the more costly truck hauling. In 2007 Quinn and Fuller placed a bid valued at more than $350 million to take the publicly traded company private.

The same year that Quinn and Fuller started their trucking company, David and Jacqueline Parker founded Covenant Transport, with only 25 tractors and 50 trailers. Today, the Chattanooga-based company belongs to a consolidated group of transportation providers offering transportation services throughout the United States. Operating a fleet of 3,700 tractors and 9,800 trailers, the company undertook a realignment to improve its competitive position in 2006. The five major new transportation divisions include Team XL (Xpedited Longhaul) service, with approximately 950 tractors, and Regional/Over the Road Solo Service, with approximately 1,125 tractors.

This page and opposite page, left: Generator at Douglas Dam in Kodak, Tennessee, operated by the Tennessee Valley Authority. Opposite page, right: Browns Ferry Nuclear Unit One in Athens, Alabama, one of three plants operated from the TVA's Chattanooga offices.

Warehousing and distribution services are the specialty of Kenco Logistic Services, a subsidiary of Kenco Group, a family-owned company founded in 1950 in Chattanooga by Jim Kennedy Jr. and Sam Smartt. The company has grown from a single warehouse and two employees to 90 facilities with more than 21 million square feet of warehouse space in 23 states and Canada. Servicing such leading companies as GlaxoSmithKline, Bristol-Myers Squibb, and Whirlpool, Kenco offers a broad range of services, from warehousing and distribution, real estate management, and transportation management to such value-added services as labeling and packaging and more.

Go Power

One of the more innovative ideas to come out of Franklin Roosevelt's New Deal was the Tennessee Valley Authority (TVA), a federal corporation established in 1933 to address problems ranging from flood control to improving crop yields to power production. Over the ensuing decades, the TVA proved itself to be as nimble and innovative as any major corporation, providing electricity to homes and businesses in a seven-state, 80,000-square-mile area—including most of Tennessee and parts of Alabama, Georgia, Kentucky, Mississippi, North Carolina, and Virginia.

Today the TVA provides electric power that is both reliable and affordable to 158 local distributors, which in turn service 8.7 million people and 650,000 businesses and industries. The TVA generates more electricity than any other public utility in the nation; it has 11 coal-fired and eight combustion-turbine plants, along with three nuclear plants, 29 hydroelectric dams, and 16 solar-power sites. In 2007 the Browns Ferry Nuclear Unit One became the first nuclear unit to be brought online in the United States in the new millennium.

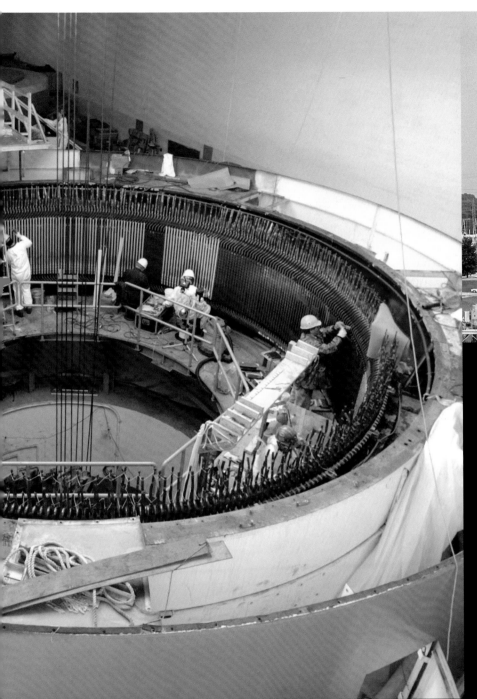

Financially self-supporting, operating without taxpayer subsidies, the TVA relies on its revenues, which exceed $9 billion a year, along with bonds, notes, and other forms of borrowing, to finance its operations. TVA bonds and notes, purchased by investors from all 50 states, have received a AAA credit rating, the highest possible rating, from Standard & Poor's, Moody's, and Fitch.

The TVA's economic impact on the region has exceeded even that which Roosevelt's New Deal had envisioned. In 2006 more than 50,000 jobs were created or retained in the region through TVA's economic development investments, which leveraged $4.2 billion in capital investment from other sources. In 2006, the TVA's tax-equivalent payments to state and local governments in eight states totaled a record $376 million.

The TVA is also environmentally responsible. Through an aggressive clean-air program, the TVA since 1977 has reduced its sulfur dioxide emissions by 80 percent and, since 1995, its nitrogen-oxide emissions by 81 percent. The TVA will have spent by 2010 an estimated $5.8 billion on clean-air modifications to its 11 coal-burning plants. In addition, the TVA's 34 flood-control dams along the Tennessee River and its tributaries help to prevent an estimated $231 million in flood damage per year.

This page: EPB lineman. Opposite page: EPB Telecom expert working with fiber-optic cable.

One of the TVA's customers is EPB, of Chattanooga. Established in 1935, EPB is one of the nation's largest publicly owned suppliers of electric power and serves more than 163,000 residents and businesses in a 600-square-mile area that includes greater Chattanooga, along with surrounding counties in Georgia and Tennessee. EPB's customers who are concerned about the environment can purchase blocks of "green power"—energy generated from renewable sources such as solar energy, wind, and methane—through the TVA's Green Power Switch program. Each block purchased is the equivalent of planting an acre of trees or recycling 883 pounds of newspapers or 240 pounds of aluminum cans. The EPB Power Share program allows customers to contribute directly to the monthly electric bills of local families in need through United Way 211, an outreach program.

Natural gas, a clean, efficient alternative to electricity, is provided by Chattanooga Gas, a subsidiary of Atlanta-based AGL Resources. Dating back to the late 1800s, Chattanooga Gas delivers around 20 billion cubic feet of gas per year to approximately 60,000 customers in Chattanooga and neighboring communities. Water for the Chattanooga area is supplied by Tennessee American Water, a wholly owned subsidiary of American Water. Founded in 1886 as American Water Works and Guarantee Company, American Water is the largest investor-owned water and wastewater utility company in the United States, providing clean water and wastewater to approximately 16.2 million people in 32 states and Ontario, Canada. Most of the nearly 6,900 employees live in the communities that they serve.

In Touch with the World

A new kind of power, one fueling innovation and growth in the 21st century, is communications. In 2000 EPB helped to bring the greater Chattanooga area into the information age with the founding of its EPB Telecom division, which within five years was providing 2,300 customers with reliable, affordable telecom service. EPB Telecom's all-fiber Internet solution, launched in 2003, provides up to 500 Mbps of bandwidth, which is nearly 300 times faster than a standard DSL, cable, or T1 connection.

Covista Communications, originally Total-Tel, moved its headquarters to Chattanooga in 2002. In addition to long-distance service, it also provides Internet and data-networking services and commercial and residential telecommunications to customers in a multistate area, including Georgia and Tennessee. Plans are under way for expansion of its residential service, the fastest-growing segment of its business.

Chattanooga residents can catch the Tennessee Titans and other favorite sports teams on cable television provided by Comcast Cable Communications. With more than 23 million subscribers, the Philadelphia-based company is one of the nation's leading providers of cable services. In addition to cable television, it also offers high-speed Internet and digital phone service.

A so-called "Baby Bell" until it was acquired by telecom giant AT&T in 2006, BellSouth Corporation provides local telephone service for nine states, including Tennessee. The first Baby Bell to be granted regulatory approval to offer long-distance service to its customers, BellSouth today has 6.5 million long-distance customers. Benefiting from AT&T's large-scale operations, BellSouth has consolidated its operations to focus on wireless and broadband services, expanding its DSL services and teaming up with DIRECTV to make satellite television available to its customers.

With the merger of the two telecom giants, BellSouth Park, the home of the Chattanooga Lookouts, a Southern League minor league baseball team, was renamed AT&T Field in 2007. Said Chattanooga Mayor Ron Littlefield, "The renaming underscores that the new AT&T is continuing the tradition of local community involvement."

That traditions can be preserved even as technological advances and economic growth are embraced bodes well for the future of Chattanooga. With clean, efficient power, a thriving trucking industry, expanding air service, and state-of-the-art telecommunications, the Chattanooga area is well-positioned to move forward in the coming decades.

PART TWO
SUCCESS STORIES:
PROFILES OF COMPANIES AND ORGANIZATIONS

Banking and
Financial Services
Cornerstone Community Bank,
    80–81

Construction, Development,
and Real Estate Services
CBL & Associates Properties, Inc., 85
ERMC, 84

Education
Covenant College, 90

Southern Adventist University,
    88–89

Insurance Services
BlueCross BlueShield of Tennessee,
    Inc., 96–97
Unum, 94–95

Health Care and Biotechnology
Erlanger Health System, 102–03
Memorial Health Care System,
    100–01

Hospitality and Tourism
Chattanooga Choo Choo, 106–07

Manufacturing and
Consumer Products
Double-Cola Co.–USA, 120–21
East Tech Company, 118–19
Hamilton Plastics, Inc., 116–17
Heil Environmental, 112–13
McKee Foods Corporation, 114–15
Propex Inc., 110–11
Sofix Corporation, 122

Professional and
Business Services
Chattanooga Manufacturers
    Association, 129
Hazlett, Lewis & Bieter, PLLC, 126–27
Joseph Decosimo and Company,
    PLLC, 128

Utilities and Telecommunications
Comcast Cable Communications,
    Inc., 132–35
EPB, 136

CBL & Associates Properties, Inc.

As one of the nation's largest mall real estate investment trusts (REITs), this dynamic Chattanooga company engages in the ownership, development, acquisition, leasing, management, and operation of properties from coast to coast, including more than 80 market-dominant shopping malls and open-air centers.

Headquartered in Chattanooga, CBL & Associates Properties, Inc. is one of the largest and most active owners and developers of malls and shopping centers in the United States. CBL owns, holds interests in, or manages more than 130 properties in 26 states, including more than 80 market-dominant enclosed malls and open-air centers. The company's growth strategy includes the development and redevelopment of premier retail destinations throughout the country as well as acquisitions.

By delivering on its promises and understanding the needs of its business partners, CBL has earned the trust of the nation's top retailers. CBL's impressive track record can be traced to the company's outstanding partnerships with retailers and a commitment to serving the community.

In 1978, the company's chairman and CEO, Charles B. Lebovitz, and five partners including John Foy, CFO, and Ben Landress, executive vice president, founded CBL to develop regional malls and community centers. Their first mall development, Plaza

del Sol in Del Rio, Texas, opened in 1979. By 1988, CBL celebrated the opening of a regional office near Boston, Massachusetts, to oversee the rapidly expanding development business in the New England region. In 1993, CBL was listed on the New York Stock Exchange (NYSE: CBL) as a real estate investment trust (REIT). Another milestone came two years later, in 1995, when CBL completed its first acquisition—WestGate Mall in Spartanburg, South Carolina.

A National and International Reach

CBL's largest acquisition took place in 2001, when the company purchased

23 properties from a commercial real estate developer, The Jacobs Group of Cleveland, Ohio. CBL's 2004 opening of a regional mall on the East Coast—Coastal Grand–Myrtle Beach in Myrtle Beach, South Carolina— and its 2005 opening of Imperial Valley Mall in El Centro, California, gave the company a coast-to-coast footprint. With continued interest in growing its nationwide portfolio of properties, the company opened a second regional office in Dallas, Texas, in 2006.

With its growing portfolio in the United States, the company began looking for opportunities to complement this growth by expanding abroad.

In 2006, CBL announced its first international investment with a mall operator and real estate developer in China. The company will continue to pursue other opportunities to further expand its international presence.

With its bold leadership, dedicated professionals, and enduring partnerships, the company is well positioned for success. In 2008 and in the future, CBL & Associates Properties, Inc. will continue its multipronged approach to strategic growth through new developments, redevelopments, acquisitions, and international opportunities in order to continue its record of enhancing shareholder value.

Above left: In its beloved home city and state of Chattanooga, Tennessee, CBL & Associates Properties, Inc.—with a national and international reach—owns and manages the state's largest regional mall, Hamilton Place, and employs hundreds of professionals at CBL Center (shown here). Above right: Charles B. Lebovitz (shown here) and five partners founded CBL in 1978 to develop regional malls and community centers.

PROFILES OF COMPANIES AND ORGANIZATIONS
Education

Southern Adventist University

This Christian university offers more than 70 undergraduate and seven master's degree programs to a student body of more than 2,600, about 25 percent of which concentrates on nursing, with campus chaplains to lead students in ministries, outreach programs, and missions abroad.

Since 1892, Southern Adventist University has prepared students for careers, service, and life.

Affiliated with the Seventh-day Adventist Church, Southern offers more than 70 undergraduate degrees and seven master's degrees in a welcoming Christian environment. The majority of Southern's students live in residence halls or apartments on the university's 1,000-acre campus, where learning takes place both inside and outside the classroom.

Recognized by *U.S.News & World Report* as a top-tier college, by The Princeton Review as one of the best colleges in the Southeast, and by *Campus Technology* magazine as a Campus Technology 2006 Innovator, Southern is accredited by the Southern Association of Colleges and Schools as well as several other specialized accrediting organizations.

Nearly a quarter of Southern's more than 2,600 students study nursing in a program that began on campus more than 50 years ago. Rapid growth within the School of Nursing has led to the construction of a new building to house

programs for associate's, bachelor's, and master's degree students. With nearly 100 percent of nursing students passing their licensure exams on the first try, Southern holds claim to one of the highest passing rates in the nation.

Many students credit the personal involvement of their professors as one of the reasons for their success. With a 16-to-one student-teacher ratio, students across campus receive personal guidance and instruction from their professors.

Students also have the opportunity to participate in research with professors. For example, physics students have benefited from working with research professor Ray Hefferlin, who has contributed groundbreaking work in the field of chemotopology by extending the periodic table to include two- and three-atom molecules.

Recreational Hot Spot

Southern's campus is home to miles of hiking trails, a natural rock-climbing wall, a cave, and a ropes course. Faculty and students from the university's outdoor education program

Right: Southern Adventist University's 1,000-acre campus, located in Collegedale, Tennessee, is an ideal location for learning, recreation, and service.

use these and other local resources to provide area schools and organizations with adventure-based programs.

The community also benefits from recreation and wellness activities provided by students and faculty from

the School of Physical Education, Health, and Wellness. The number of activities available to the community is expanding with the construction of the Hulsey Wellness Center, a state-of-the-art complex that includes a heated therapy pool, an indoor rock-climbing wall, workout

facilities, and an indoor track. The new wellness center also includes a specialized gymnasium for Southern's antidrug acrobatic team, the Gym-Masters.

Cultural Contributor
Southern's School of Music hosts several student musical groups that perform locally and on tours. These include a symphony orchestra, a wind symphony, a jazz ensemble, and several choral groups.

The campus is also home to a 70-stop Brombaugh tracker organ. Three students who studied on this organ under the direction of Professor Judy Glass have received Fulbright Scholarships.

In addition to providing the community with classical music and community information, Southern's radio station, WSMC, has partnered with Read 20 to read on the air to children for 20 minutes each Thursday.

Secret of the Cave, a feature film created by Southern's School of Visual Art and Design with assistance from students and faculty, was presented a Crystal Heart Award at the Heartland Film Festival in 2006 and selected for the 2007 Santa Barbara Film Festival. The School of Visual Art and Design also has dedicated art exhibit space to display student work.

Another cultural gem on campus is Southern's Lynn H. Wood Archaeological Museum. This award-winning museum is home to one of the largest teaching collections of Near East artifacts in the United States and is open to the public for free tours.

Active in Service
The vibrant Christian atmosphere on Southern's campus is apparent in the many opportunities throughout the week for students to gather for worship or Bible study. Two full-time chaplains and a student chaplain assistant lead the students in countless ministries and outreach programs, including a student missions program that sends more than 100 students around the world each year to serve in various capacities.

Students and faculty serve as volunteers in various community outreach and assistance programs, culminating in an annual Community Service Day when more than a third of the student body and faculty serve at area nonprofit organizations.

Through programs like these, Southern is making a difference in Chattanooga and the world. More importantly, students' lives are forever being changed by the friendships, ideas, and experiences they encounter at Southern. These students often go on to serve as leaders in their careers, communities, and churches.

Southern Adventist University provides additional information on its Web site (www.southern.edu).

Above left: A 16-to-one student-faculty ratio means graduate and undergraduate students alike receive personalized attention from their professors. Above center: Friends pausing to pray together is a common sight on this Christian campus. Above right: The natural rock-climbing wall provides one of many recreational opportunities on Southern's campus.

Covenant College

This esteemed liberal arts college, which spans some 300 acres on scenic Lookout Mountain, ranks among the top seven colleges in the South. Covenant College provides a rigorous, Christ-centered education in the liberal arts to over 1,250 students.

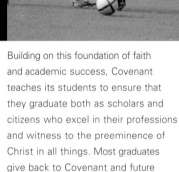

Above left: More than 50 areas of study are available to Covenant College students, who go on to succeed at the highest levels of virtually every discipline. With a low student-to-faculty ratio, each student benefits from individual attention from nationally respected professors. Above center: Located on beautiful Lookout Mountain, Covenant College is just minutes from downtown Chattanooga and enjoys many ties with the local community. Above right: Covenant offers men's and women's varsity athletic programs in baseball, basketball, cross-country, golf, soccer, softball, tennis, and volleyball.

Building on this foundation of faith and academic success, Covenant teaches its students to ensure that they graduate both as scholars and citizens who excel in their professions and witness to the preeminence of Christ in all things. Most graduates give back to Covenant and future students through the alumni program.

In recent years, Covenant College has seen a steady increase in admissions and expects this trend to continue. To keep pace with this growth, the college is increasing its academic offerings and expanding its infrastructure. Recent capital projects include construction of a new residence hall and academic building, as well as renovation of the library and continued development of athletic facilities and the campus green. Plans are underway for renovation of Covenant's flagship building, Carter Hall.

While providing students with a stimulating environment in which they can learn and strengthen their faith, Covenant College also creates a promising future for graduates who will make a difference in the Chattanooga area and beyond.

Since its move to Lookout Mountain in 1964, Covenant College has contributed to the intellectual, spiritual, cultural, and economic life of the greater Chattanooga area.

Today more than 1,250 students from 47 states and 17 countries around the world take advantage of the top-notch education at Covenant College, just minutes from downtown Chattanooga. From a sprawling campus that spans some 300 acres on scenic Lookout Mountain, this liberal arts college offers associate's, bachelor's, and master's degrees, as well as several preprofessional programs.

Covenant College offers a low student-to-faculty ratio, and the vast majority of its professors hold doctorate or terminal degrees. The school's most popular majors are English, history, education, business, and psychology. Covenant's 12 varsity athletic teams have a history of success, with some advancing to national tournaments in recent years.

Many graduates stay in the Chattanooga area after finishing their degrees. Alumni are currently employed at Chattanooga-area businesses, hospitals, accounting firms, real estate companies, and many other organizations. Covenant graduates also have founded such

local businesses as technology firms and restaurants, which contribute to the growth and development of the greater Chattanooga area.

Excellence in Higher Education

The mission of Covenant, which was founded in 1955, has been constant—to provide its students a rigorous, Christ-centered education, equipping them to contribute to their communities and professions. Entering students profess their Christian faith and have a solid academic background. The college is accredited by the Commission on Colleges of the Southern Association of Colleges and Schools.

Covenant College

PROFILES OF COMPANIES AND ORGANIZATIONS
Insurance Services

Unum

This Fortune 250 corporation based in Chattanooga provides more than 100,000 businesses—representing 21 million American workers—with innovative employee benefits and services. With $10.5 billion in revenues, Unum contributes generously to a wide variety of community organizations.

Left: Unum executives celebrate the company's new brand identity. From left are Robert C. Greving, executive vice president and CFO; Kathy Owen, chief information officer; Rhonda Rigsby, vice president of compensation; Timothy Arnold, vice president of regional underwriting; Charles Tinker, vice president of broker compensation services; Brent Rogers, chief technology officer; and David Fussell, senior vice president of investments. Right, top: Employees, from left, Davis Nichols, Kimberly Sanford, and Vicki Y. Simmons show their new Unum badges. Right, bottom: The home offices of Unum are located in Chattanooga.

Despite its recognized position as a leading employee benefits provider in the United States and United Kingdom, Unum sees itself simply as "people serving people."

Thomas R. Watjen, Unum president and CEO, elaborates, "Our services and benefits are designed to help people during a difficult time when they are suffering from a loss of income due to illness or injury. However, we provide more than just a benefit check to claimants. Unum also is about helping employers as much as their employees."

Today, Unum provides benefit programs to more than 100,000 businesses, which translates into protecting some 21 million people. It is the nation's number one provider of disability insurance and long-term care, and among the top three carriers in group life and voluntary workplace benefits.

Unum's success can be attributed to its simple yet direct philosophy regarding claims. It begins with a thorough, fair, and objective evaluation of all claims to determine an appropriate decision. Once a claim is assessed and verified, Unum will pay benefits in a timely manner with a high level of service. Finally, Unum partners with its customers to help them return to work or independent living.

Heritage of Service

This philosophy has been the underpinning of the company since its creation as Provident Life and Accident Insurance Company in 1887 in Chattanooga. In 1998 the company merged with Unum Corporation, and it continues to set the pace of the industry with product and service innovations in employee benefits.

Still headquartered in Chattanooga, Unum has offices located around the country—in Portland, Maine; Worcester, Massachusetts; Glendale, California; and Columbia, South Carolina. Of its 10,000 employees worldwide, 3,000 are in Chattanooga, making Unum one of the city's largest employers.

Innovative Approach

Innovation is a hallmark of Unum, and it starts with the company's approach to meeting employers' needs. Unum combines benefit

choices, simplified administration, and cost-effective solutions that are integrated in one package to meet employees' diverse needs at different stages of life and financial situations.

While Unum can provide employees with a variety of benefit options, it also minimizes administration and eliminates redundancy and work for employers. The company uses state-of-the-art computer systems and is staffed by knowledgeable professionals to streamline the workflow process from enrollment to plan administration through claims processing.

"We believe that good benefits are good business—for any employer," says Watjen. "Our goal is to provide benefit plans that help employees while helping companies build stronger workforces and ultimately more profitable businesses."

The competition to recruit and retain employees along with rising health care costs and changing workforce demographics create a challenging environment for employers of all sizes. Unum understands these challenges. It offers a range of robust, cost-effective benefit solutions that meet the needs of any organization. It can create flexible benefit packages that are company-funded, employee-funded, or shared to stretch an employer's benefits budget.

Community Benefits

As a leading benefits company, Unum is committed to its claimants, employers, employees, shareholders, and communities. Over the years, it has generously lived up to this commitment. In 2006 it contributed more than $5.4 million to nonprofit organizations throughout the United States and United Kingdom, including $2.2 million to United Way.

In fact, Unum is the largest contributor to United Way in southeast Tennessee. It also provides significant support to Allied Arts, the Siskin Hospital for Rehabilitation, the Siskin Children's Institute, and Big Brothers Big Sisters. Unum's headquarters in Chattanooga has served as a temporary gallery for local art through the Association for Visual Arts (AVA) Art in the Workplace program. Exhibits feature original artwork by professional artists in the area.

Through the company's matching gifts program, in 2006 Unum employees in Chattanooga contributed $600,000 to area schools and community organizations. In line with its commitment to public education, Unum also supports Junior Achievement and the Chattanooga–Hamilton County Bicentennial Library's reading program for children ages three to five.

Watjen sums up his company's community involvement this way: "We have a responsibility to not only offer exceptional products and services to our customers but also to be a company that benefits the communities in which our employees live and work. I am proud of Unum's accomplishments and look forward to continuing our progress."

Above left: Unum's Marketing Communications and Voluntary Products team includes, from left, Ingrid Dysinger, Fred Wiechmann, Valarie Swafford, Jason Brown, and Leslie Rains. Above right: Sally White, business change and implementation analyst, volunteers at Brown Academy in Chattanooga, helping students with Junior Achievement's "JA in a Day" activities.

BlueCross BlueShield of Tennessee, Inc.

An innovative and customer-focused provider of health care plans, this not-for-profit independent company is positioned to transform the health care delivery system by increasing its efficiency, effectiveness, and affordability in Tennessee and on a national level.

Above left: BlueCross BlueShield of Tennessee, Inc. (BCBST) maintains company headquarters at its Chattanooga campus. Above right: Vicky Gregg serves as president and CEO of BCBST.

In more than 60 years, the purpose of BlueCross BlueShield of Tennessee, Inc. (BCBST) has not changed—to provide peace of mind to company customers and members. With annual revenues of more than $3 billion and regional offices in Jackson, Johnson City, Knoxville, Memphis, and Nashville, Tennessee, BCBST is a leading player in the state's health care industry. Leveraging that strength, BCBST is focused on transforming the health care delivery system both in Tennessee and on a national scale. The end goal of this transformation is a patient-centered, value-based, and affordable health care system for all.

Transforming Health Care

Since 1945, BCBST's mission has been to offer its clients peace of mind through affordable solutions for health and healing, life and living. Those solutions are delivered statewide and nationally through the company's 13 subsidiaries and affiliates, which administer group, individual, Medicare, and Medicaid plans, as well as other insurance services including life, disability, long-term care, and dental coverage.

Underlying these programs is the company belief that transformational change is needed to increase the efficiency, effectiveness, and affordability of health care. Transformation is defined as a shift in focus from process to outcomes, from administration to results, and from volume to impact. BCBST outlines five critical steps for implementing industry change:

- **Enhanced Consumer-Directed Focus:** To empower consumers through knowledge and information that will help them achieve better outcomes, including health plan comparisons, treatment costs, and information regarding hospital and physician costs and quality
- **Product Innovation:** To continue to develop unique insurance products that offer flexibility and choice and that go beyond simply delivering the best networks, and to innovate a menu of choices for the modern work environment
- **Expanded Health Information Technology:** To leverage information technology by creating the largest electronic exchange of health care data for the Medicaid population, and to ensure that clinicians have the information they need to treat patients at the point of care
- **Integrated Health Management:** To focus on total care management that keeps people healthy by providing members with preventive measures as the best insurance and care coordination to manage current medical conditions to positively impact health outcomes

- **Value-Based Reimbursement:** To recognize and reward excellent performance by those who achieve administrative efficiencies, improve clinical quality, and enhance patient satisfaction

Moving Forward with Operational and Financial Strength

The whole of BCBST's Government business—including TennCare and Medicare—serves nearly three million members in all 95 counties in Tennessee, and provides services to more than five million people nationwide, including Medicare Operations.

BCBST enjoys solid financial strength that includes healthy reserves and strong credit ratings from nationally recognized institutions. These strengths are indicative of BCBST's commitment to business excellence and long-term

viability, and they establish a solid foundation for future growth and innovation. In addition, BCBST's top-tier customer satisfaction and member retention rates set a standard among industry competitors.

Supporting Its Subsidiary Companies

Within Tennessee and beyond, BCBST is working to meet the immediate and future challenges of an increasingly complex and competitive health care industry.

Shared Health is one example of a company subsidiary working to empower consumers through knowledge and information. Shared Health is a revolutionary record-keeping system that is designed to transform the health care system and eliminate the paper-intensive medical records process.

Shared Health also connects patients, doctors, and other health care workers with the most advanced digital patient records from a single, secured online source. By working with patients, doctors, employers, and insurers, BCBST is confident that

its 21st-century solutions will lead to better communication, better care, less waste, and a more efficient system.

Ensuring Medicare Services

Riverbend Government Benefits Administrator, another subsidiary of BCBST and a provider of Part A services to more than 3,400 Medicare providers across the United States, is committed to serving seniors. Riverbend is the largest payer of Medicare claims in America's freestanding rural health clinics. Riverbend, which is also the national intermediary between the Centers for Medicare & Medicaid Services, paid $21 million in benefits in 2006.

The BCBST subsidiary Gordian Health Solutions focuses on wellness initiatives that are garnering national attention and have the potential to change the health care industry. As studies increasingly point to the negative impact of stress and other health issues on worker productivity, Gordian is producing bottom line results for customers by helping their employees lead healthier lives.

BCBST is the insurer or administrator for all of the state's Cover Tennessee programs through the Volunteer State Health Plan, Inc. (VSHP) subsidiary. Several different insurance products are available through Cover Tennessee. CoverKids offers comprehensive health insurance in Tennessee to uninsured children ages 18 and under and to pregnant women. AccessTN provides a comprehensive health insurance plan for seriously ill adults who have been denied coverage by insurance companies.

CoverTN partners with the state, private employers, and individuals to offer guaranteed, affordable, limited health coverage for uninsured employees of Tennessee's small businesses. CoverRx offers affordable medication to low-income, uninsured residents of the state. Both programs were created to help Tennesseans gain better access to health care.

Contributing to Its Communities

In 2006 BCBST contributed nearly $5 million to Tennessee communities through the BlueCross BlueShield of Tennessee Health Foundation, Inc.; through the BlueCross BlueShield of Tennessee Community Trust; and through other corporate donations and in-kind gifts.

A strong and sustainable core business, an actionable plan for innovative growth, a dynamic and engaged senior leadership, and a community focus provide the complete picture of BCBST—a company that is energized, vital, and committed to customers, clients, employees, and the broader communities that it serves. BlueCross BlueShield of Tennessee, Inc. is a place where nearly 5,000 employees can be proud of what they do and where they work.

Above: BCBST is improving efficiency and lowering costs by consolidating its administrative operations at its corporate headquarters on Cameron Hill in downtown Chattanooga. This new office complex is projected for completion in 2009. Shown in this rendering is the design for the facility's courtyard.

PROFILES OF COMPANIES AND ORGANIZATIONS
Manufacturing and Consumer Products

Propex Inc.

This global company manufactures and markets engineered fibers and fabrics used as geosynthetics, concrete reinforcement, furnishings, and for other applications. It provides customers with quality service and expertise, from ordering to product installation, and continuously strives to protect the environment.

As a pioneer in the development and manufacture of a multitude of products used every day by people around the globe, Propex Inc. is the world's largest independent manufacturer of woven and nonwoven polypropylene fabrics for carpet backing and bedding, as well as fibers for concrete reinforcement. It is also the premier global supplier of geo-textile fabrics, erosion-control mats, and other products for industrial applications such as building products, furniture, packaging, filtration, pool covers, and automotive interiors.

As a leader in research and market edu-cation in its field, Propex is the creator of such well-known brands as ActionBac® carpet backings; Pyramat® high-perform-ance turf reinforcement mats (HPTRMs); Fibermesh® concrete reinforcement; Duon® nonwovens; and ArmorMax™, one of the most advanced technologies to protect earthen levees from storm surges and wave-overtopping erosion.

In addition to its headquarters and manufacturing facilities in Chattanooga, the company also operates U.S. plants in Bainbridge, Hazlehurst, Ringgold, Alto, and Nashville, Georgia. All of these facilities operate under the Propex Quality Advantage, which is a promise to "consistently treat every customer's business as though it were their own." To fulfill this promise, Propex maintains a uniform quality system that focuses on a defect-free environment in all of its processes, from the time of ordering to the delivery to market. For its accom-plishments in these and other areas, Propex is one of a select group of con-struction material companies to achieve ISO–9001:2000 certification, which is given by the International Organization for Standardization.

Additionally, Propex has sales offices, factories, distribution centers, and tech-nical support in countries worldwide, including Germany, Brazil, Hungary, Mexico, and the United Kingdom. European operations follow strict manu-facturing specifications, quality control monitoring, and laboratory testing to meet or exceed European standards.

History and Strategic Expansion

Propex's predecessor company began in 1884 as Patchogue Mills, a producer of curtains, tablecloths, handkerchiefs, rope, and twine. When the company acquired Plymouth Rug Mills in 1919, the business was structured as two divisions, International Handkerchief and Patchogue Plymouth Mills. In the 1940s Patchogue Plymouth Mills acquired the Hodges Fiber Company and expanded to include a jute- and kraftcord- (tightly twisted plant-fiber cord used to make backing yarn) weaving operation in north Georgia. This marked the beginning of Patchogue Plymouth Mills' alignment with carpet manufacturers and its devel-opment of new weaving yarns and back-ings for the flooring industry.

In the 1960s Patchogue Plymouth Mills began manufacturing polypropylene yarn. Around this time the company was acquired by Amoco. It became Amoco Fabrics and Fibers, and its

the company's products while supporting the Tennessee Aquarium, Creative Discovery Museum, the Chattanooga Nature Center, the Riverbend Festival's Faith & Family Night, and the Chattanooga Lookouts, as well as numerous smaller projects.

Family funds provided the Ruth McKee Mission Control classroom at the Challenger Center on the campus of the University of Tennessee at Chattanooga (UTC). The Challenger Center simulates space missions for teachers and students. It is named in Ruth's honor because near the end of her life she expressed regret that her years of teaching had been so few. The family also funded a chair of excellence for the study of dyslexia at UTC to honor O. D. McKee. His example of triumph over dyslexia is an inspiration to young people who fear that their learning disability might keep them from being successful.

McKee Foods is also a major contributor to United Way of Greater Chattanooga, encouraging employees to contribute, loaning the services of an executive each year, and giving a generous corporate gift.

Family-Owned with Family Commitment

McKee Foods, then as now, remains family-owned, and members of the third generation of McKees now lead the company. The McKees have been proactive in avoiding the pitfalls that have caused other family-owned companies to go from private to public ownership in their generation. They know that family ownership is another of the "better ways" that their grandparents so often talked about. Employees also benefit—family businesses can ride out fluctuations in the market, do not have frequent changes in leadership, and provide stability in the business world.

Privately held, family-owned businesses have the ability to make decisions that are best for the long-term good of the company. Although automation initiatives and plant expansions require McKee Foods to commit considerable funds to capital investment, the owners know that long-term goals of improving productivity and growing sales require it.

The Customer Is King

Customer satisfaction with McKee Foods products and service helps the company grow. The goal of McKee Foods is to manufacture products that are consistent from shift to shift and location to location. Maintaining consistently high quality standards is one way that this company makes its products stand out. Research and development is

also important in a company convinced that providing a wide range of products is another of the secrets of McKee Foods' success.

The Future

McKee Foods has been profitable every year since the late 1950s, partly because of its can-do attitude and optimism about the future. The company continues to expand plants, increase automation, and develop new products with the goal of future sustainability and profitability.

O. D. and Ruth McKee, who died in 1995 and 1989, respectively, would be proud that their children and grandchildren value their legacy and continue to invest time and money in the business, which was such a major part of the founders' lives and so dear to their hearts.

Above left: McKee Foods Corporation has grown to be one of the largest employers in the greater Chattanooga area. Growth, a hallmark of McKee Foods' history, continues today. Apison Plant in Collegedale is undergoing a major expansion that will nearly double the size and capacity of the facility. Above right: McKee Foods produces more than 160 different varieties of Little Debbie® snack products. The Oatmeal Creme Pie® was the original consumer favorite and remains just as popular today.

Hamilton Plastics, Inc.

One of Chattanooga's most admired companies, this manufacturer conducts research and creates advanced plastic films and bags for industries such as poultry and other food processing, medical, foam, and housing. It credits its success to its loyalty, quality, and personal attention in serving customers' needs.

Above: The 300,000-square-foot Hamilton Plastics, Inc. complex, located in Centre South Riverport Industrial Park in Chattanooga, houses state-of-the-art facilities for the manufacturing of industrial films and bags. For employees, there is a picnic pavilion and a health club on the premises.

Loyalty, quality, and personal attention are the hallmarks of Hamilton Plastics, Inc., a Chattanooga-based manufacturer of food-packaging bags and lamination films. Loyalty to and from employees, customers, and suppliers has contributed to the company's growth; quality is the by-product of Hamilton Plastics' advanced research and development capability, which enables the creation of monolayer and multilayer coextruded products; and personal attention is given to every aspect of the operation by company owner and CEO Harshad Shah.

Shah's dreams of starting a company began as a youth when he came to the United States from India to further his education. He devoted 18 hours a day to his work and studies and was always looking for an opportunity to start a technical business. His first endeavor was a small testing and consulting firm, which led to his decision to introduce a new product to the marketplace.

Shah founded Hamilton Plastics in 1986 with a small group of investors, one extruder, one bag machine, and zero orders. The company was located in a 24,000-square-foot building, from which it began steadily manufacturing a wide assortment of plastic bags and film for industrial applications, food processing, the medical industry, and other specialized industries in need of value-added, coextruded products.

One of the company's greatest accomplishments is the development and application of technologically advanced wrapping—leading to the creation of a plastic bag for the poultry industry that keeps products fresh for 21 days without freezing. Pilgrim's Pride, one of the largest chicken-processing companies in the United States and a client of Hamilton Plastics, has been a key customer, helping the company's growth. Other factors in the success of Hamilton Plastics include being approved by the National Minority Supplier Development Council (NMSDC) as a certified minority-owned business enterprise.

Two Decades of Growth

Five years after its inception, Hamilton Plastics needed more space, which in 1991 spurred the company to build a state-of-the-art plant. The five-acre site was chosen because it would accommodate future expansion with minimal cost. Growth continued throughout the 1990s; in 1999 five more acres were purchased, doubling the size of the Hamilton Plastics complex. This expansion included an additional research and testing facility and a health club for employees.

In 2003 Hamilton Plastics acquired an additional six acres, adding a 40,000-square-foot building as well as a picnic pavilion for employees and doubling rail access to a total of 800 feet. In 2006 the company celebrated more than 20 years in business with a $14.5 million expansion of its plant, which is located in the Centre South Riverport Industrial Park, adding 160,000 square feet for an overall operation of 300,000 square feet.

This expansion added another two coextrusion lines to Hamilton Plastics' 20 existing lines—enabling the business to meet increasing customer demand

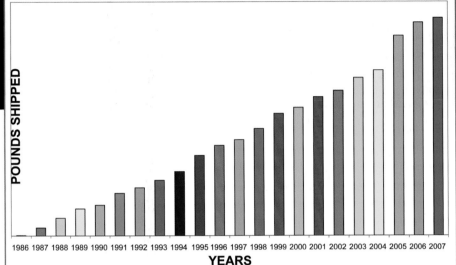

for value-added products that save time and money. It also created 25 new jobs, bringing the company's total employment to 160 people.

An Outstanding Employer

Shah believes that loyalty is as important to the company's success as the quality of the products it sells. His loyalty to suppliers, customers, and employees is as strong as his loyalty to his own family. His business philosophy is that greed yields short-term gains that only bring an unpleasant end. Shah's concern for employees has brought its own gift of loyalty in return. Many of the company's original employees are still on board two decades later, serving as the backbone of the company's management and manufacturing teams. Their

dedication and commitment to the company's strong beliefs cultivate the environment necessary to attract both new employees and new customers, continuing the tradition of growth and success.

Highly trained technicians, operators, customer service personnel, and sales and service representatives demonstrate the company's special brand of loyalty and commitment to hard work, high quality, and dependable service.

A Small-Business Star

Hamilton Plastics sets an excellent example for other small businesses with its reputation as an exemplary employer and its dedication to the highest standards for quality products

and manufacturing processes. The company has been the winner of the Chattanooga Area Chamber of Commerce Small Business Award and the Chattanooga American Business Ethics Award, and in 2003 it was named a finalist for the coveted Kruesi Award for Innovation. The company has also been recognized as one of the top 100 manufacturers in the nation by *Plastics News* magazine.

Shah feels that Chattanooga is a great environment for business, especially small business. He credits local city and county governments for their support and cooperation in helping business owners succeed and credits the labor force with an eagerness to learn and try new things. Hamilton Plastics' sophisticated computer equipment includes specialized laser technology that requires time and patience to master. Shah praises his employees for becoming proficient operators of this equipment.

With a hands-on approach to every aspect of the business—from managing employees and purchasing raw materials to developing products and marketing and sales—Shah has led the company

through 20 years of consistent growth, averaging 13 percent growth per year since the beginning. Hamilton Plastics and its employees look forward to continued growth, success, and leadership within the industry.

Above left: Annual figures for pounds of goods shipped are charted over more than 20 years, reflecting the consistency of the company's growth. Above right: Hamilton Plastics conducts extensive research to continually develop new techniques, materials, and product applications. Left: Technologically advanced coextrusion lines enable Hamilton Plastics to constantly improve existing products and innovatively design new products for current and new customers seeking added value.

East Tech Company

This fast-growing Chattanooga company offers precision engineering and custom-manufacturing for applications in the power generation, water treatment, automotive, textile, and medical industries. It is committed to quality and customer service and uses advanced equipment and software to meet customers' needs.

Above: East Tech Company's 30,000-square-foot facility is located in the Centre South Riverport Industrial Park, off Amnicola Highway in Chattanooga, Tennessee.

Business has doubled each year for East Tech Company since it opened its doors on January 16, 2004. President and CEO Roger Layne started the company in a 10,000-square-foot building with a $1.2 million investment and $700,000 in new, state-of-the-art equipment. The company immediately began to grow, and in February 2007 it invested in a new headquarters building that is three times the size of the original location. The facility is located in the Centre South Riverport Industrial Park, off Amnicola Highway, in Chattanooga, Tennessee.

Widely recognized in the power, hydroelectric, and nuclear industries, East Tech offers high-tech engineering and custom-manufacturing services by using the most advanced computerized numerical control (CNC) machining technology. Its five Mazak CNC machining centers, each with a 12,000-rpm spindle, are some of the fastest in the industry, and powerful software for modeling parts is used to create two-dimensional and three-dimensional geometric forms. High-speed precision equipment, documented quality systems, and a documented nuclear machining program all contribute to the products and services East Tech provides.

East Tech specializes in research and development, prototypes, and production, and can generate replacement components or take a customer's simple drawing from raw material to a finished product. The company has efficient, effective processes in place to give customers the flexibility of ordering as few or as many parts as are needed. Offering Engineering, Welding, CNC Milling, CNC Turning, Machining, Wire EDM (electrical discharge machining), and Surface Grinding specialties, East Tech has the resources to complete any secondary manufacturing process, and it also handles assembly and complete turnkey projects. In addition to providing high quality services, East Tech engages only the highest quality vendors in order to ensure 100 percent customer satisfaction. Komatsu America Corp., Alstom Power Inc., and Westinghouse Electric Company are among the clients that East Tech serves. Locally, East Tech works closely with the Tennessee Valley Authority and Astec Industries. Other clients served by East Tech include companies in the automotive, medical, and textile industries.

Behind all great companies are great employees, and East Tech is no exception. Layne understands that employees are the company's most valuable asset. He is committed to providing a productive work environment for employees, along with the essential resources they need to complete their tasks successfully. Prospective employees are interviewed several times to determine that they are well qualified for the specific

duties of the job for which they apply. All personnel undergo intensive training in the value of meeting customer needs and complying with statutory and regulatory requirements. East Tech works in partnership with Chattanooga State Technical Community College to offer local graduates an opportunity to become fully trained employees.

Along with superior performance on the technical side, East Tech also supports many community organizations. The company is a participating member of the Chattanooga Area Chamber of Commerce, Chattanooga Manufacturers Association, and the Better Business Bureau. East Tech is also a member of the National Federation of Independent Businesses. In 2005 East Tech was nominated for the Chattanooga Area Chamber of Commerce Small Business Award. In 2006 East Tech received the Fast 50 award, given by *BusinessTN* magazine, for being one of the 50 fastest-growing companies in Tennessee. East Tech also partners with Sequoyah High School in the development of their machine tool technology program. Layne serves on the Chattanooga Area Chamber of Commerce Education Committee and is an executive board member of the Chattanooga Manufacturers Association. He is also on the advisory committee of Wade Silvey's Machine Tool Technology Program at Chattanooga State Tech and Garry Nabors' Machine Tool Technology Program at Sequoyah High School.

In fewer than four years, East Tech accomplished what a company might strive for over a lifetime, and it is still growing strong. Sales in 2006 reached $2.6 million and are expected to rise at a rate of about 35 percent a year.

With room to expand in the new 30,000-square-foot facility, Layne and his team purchase new equipment each year. East Tech is adding 20 new employees in 2007 and 2008, and a Phase II expansion is planned for 2009.

Roger Layne and East Tech Company are clearly on the road to a great future. The company constantly strives to exceed customer expectations with excellence in quality and service. "Our reputation is based on what we did yesterday. Our future is determined by what we do today and tomorrow," Layne says. "Our objective is to have the best quality products and the best trained workforce in the industry."

Above, both photos: Equipped with state-of-the-art computer numerical controlled (CNC) machinery, East Tech is able to take on even the most difficult projects and customized requests.

A sip of Double-Cola is a sip of history. First as the Good Grape Company and now as Double-Cola Co.–USA, this maker of Double-Cola, Ski, Jumbo, and other beverages has been refreshing thirsty people across the country for more than 85 years. The company also makes other carbonated beverages—including Double-Dry Ginger Ale, tonic water, sparkling water mixers, Oranta, and Chaser—which are available only outside the United States.

Double-Cola and Ski, however, remain the company's mainstays.

Chattanoogans Charles D. Little and Joe S. Foster founded the company in 1922 to market a grape soda they invented called Good Grape. They soon followed it with Double-Orange. In 1924 the Good Grape Company changed its name to the Seminole Flavor Company and developed its first cola drink, Marvel Cola.

After refining the formula, the company changed Marvel's name to Jumbo Cola, selling it in seven-and-a-half-ounce bottles rather than the six-ounce bottles that were standard in the day. The company outdid itself again in 1933, perfecting its cola formula and debuting it in 12-ounce bottles that were, of course, twice the size of other major colas. These 12-ounce bottles were sold for a nickel, using the slogan "Two full glasses in every bottle. Double-Good, Double-Cola." Double-Cola appealed

to a wide range of consumers, adults and kids alike, and quickly became the company's signature soda.

Double-Cola's popularity prompted the company to change its name again in 1953, from Seminole Flavor Company to the Double-Cola Company. It continued its legacy of innovation—in 1956 it formulated Ski, a combination of natural orange and lemon juices. In 1957 it began marketing Double-Cola in 16-ounce

AIN OR SHINE

A GREAT DRINK
DOUBLE COLA
A MIGHTY FLAVOR

2 GLASSES IN THE 5¢ BOTTLE

*double measure
double pleasure*

DRINK
DOUBLE COLA

bottles, the first major soft drink company to do so. And in 1962 the company introduced Diet Way, a low-calorie version of Double-Cola. That same year, cofounder Little sold the firm to Fairmont Foods Company. The company was given its present name, Double-Cola Co.–USA, in 1980, when it was acquired by K. J. International Inc., a privately held company. Today, Double-Cola Co.–USA's product line and distribution area, both domestic

and international, continue to grow. The company's soft drinks are now enjoyed by people in multiple countries around the world.

While part of a global enterprise, Double-Cola Co.–USA remains true to its Chattanooga roots. Its products have continued to do well over the years. This is partly because the company continues to listen to its loyal fans, as when it introduced Cherry Ski in response to requests from kids in

Breese, Illinois, in 1996, and when it brought out caffeine-free Ski in 2001.

Double-Cola, Ski, and Jumbo maintain widespread popularity across the country. Ski is the official drink of Camp Joy, a Boy Scout camp in Carlyle, Illinois, that is located near the Double-Cola/Ski bottling plant in Breese. And on their Grammy-winning album *Pickin' on Nashville*, the Kentucky Headhunters sing about having "a slawburger, fries, and a

bottle of Ski" in their number-one hit song "Dumas Walker," pointing out the Bluegrass State's fondness for the brand.

Although Double-Cola Co.–USA is a global company, it has retained its origins in Chattanooga. "Chattanooga is truly a remarkable place in which to both live and conduct business," states Alnoor Dhanani, president of Double-Cola Co.–USA. "It has great civic and business leadership and an amazing community spirit."

Above left: This original advertising poster from 1942 featured the distinctive two Double-Cola servings in one five-cent bottle. Above right: "Double Measure, Double Pleasure" was one of the many unique slogans used by Double-Cola in Chattanooga.

While most people are unfamiliar with color formers, most come into contact every day with ATM receipts, cash or credit card receipts, labels, or some type of movie, stadium, or mass transit ticket. Color formers, simply stated, are chemical powders that are used to treat paper. Then an image can be formed on the treated paper by applying pressure (for carbonless paper) or heat (for thermal paper). Thermal paper is used for printing receipts, labels, and tickets and for many other applications. Chattanooga is home to the world's leading supplier of high quality color formers, Sofix Corporation.

Sofix was established as a Tennessee corporation in 1990 with one goal: to provide a stable supply of high quality color formers for makers of coated papers, initially those in the United States, and later, worldwide. The company also makes sulfuric acid for use in wastewater treatment. Since beginning manufacturing in 1992, this enterprise—a joint venture between Yamada Chemical Company, Ltd. and Nagase & Company, Ltd.—has doubled in size in both workforce and manufacturing output. It is ISO 9001 and ISO 14001 certified. In 2005 Sofix was approved as a Foreign Trade Zone client, which enhances its position as an exporter.

Coloring Success

Major paper-coating operations across the country and around the world are the primary end users of color formers. Orders are placed with Nagase, the sole customer of Sofix color formers, and are shipped by Sofix to the end user.

Hiroshi Aoki, executive vice president and treasurer, elaborates, "Both Nagase and our end users expect a dependable, high quality product that is available with short lead times and at competitive prices. We typically ship directly to the end user and treat them as our own customer."

Sofix attributes its success largely to its values. "Our primary focus is a quality product for customer satisfaction," notes Aoki. "We also strive to integrate safety in all we do and to operate in an environmentally responsible manner."

A Place in the Community

Sofix is engaged in supporting the local community. Employees serve on the boards of the YMCA Hixson branch and the University of Tennessee at Chattanooga Chemical Engineering Department, and are actively involved in Big Brothers Big Sisters. The company provides financial sponsorship for local nonprofit organizations including United Way, Orange Grove Center, and the Newspaper-in-School program, and has contributed to the capital campaign of the College of Engineering at The University of Tennessee at Chattanooga.

Sofix chose Chattanooga not only because the city was receptive to the business but also because it is geographically similar to its parent company's city, Kyoto, Japan. Over the years Sofix has discovered that the community has a highly skilled labor pool with a strong work ethic.

Aoki concludes, "We are extremely pleased with Chattanooga and the people we have hired. They have played a major part in our growth and success over the years, and we anticipate that our success will continue."

PROFILES OF COMPANIES AND ORGANIZATIONS
Professional and Business Services

Hazlett, Lewis & Bieter, PLLC

For over 60 years, this firm has provided professional services to clients in the greater Chattanooga region. Its knowledgeable staff provides accounting, auditing, business consulting, tax, and other services for financial institutions and a variety of other businesses, government agencies, and nonprofit organizations.

In the broad and perpetually evolving realm of accounting, consulting, and information technology companies, Chattanooga-based Hazlett, Lewis & Bieter, PLLC, certified public accountants and business advisors, stands out and stands strong. The firm founded by Roy Hazlett back in 1943, known today as HLB, flourishes because it maintains an unwavering commitment to integrity and it consistently delivers high quality service and applies sound business judgment.

HLB, which employs 60 people, has core specialties in accounting, tax services, auditing, and business consulting, serving local and multi-state clients. Its service territory fans out 350 miles from Chattanooga in all directions—a circle that includes the Nashville, Memphis, and Knoxville, Tennessee, and Atlanta, Georgia, metropolitan areas.

Professional Services

With its diverse service offerings, HLB has a dedicated clientele in a broad array of industries, including financial, construction, government, health care, manufacturing, nonprofit, and emerging fields. It helps clients by assessing their needs and providing solutions so that they will be in a position to achieve their strategic goals.

Economic development agencies count on firms such as HLB to help drive the region's bustling economy. Entrepreneurs want to do business where there are professional services firms that can provide support as needed, and HLB has attracted entrepreneurs to Chattanooga for more than 60 years by doing just that.

HLB has always helped entrepreneurs manage the growth of their businesses—a commitment that continues today. The firm's specialists are attuned to the special needs of companies with high rates of growth and offer expertise in business valuation, computer hardware and software systems, business plans, expanded ownership, cash flow analysis, fraud detection, and more.

As its clients' needs evolve, HLB expands its offerings—its information technology services, for instance—and continually seeks innovative ways to keep its clients competitive. To ensure that its staff is on top of the latest developing trends, HLB provides comprehensive training for new employees, and senior

staff members receive training in their area of specialty.

The firm has long had a reputation for its solid auditing practice. HLB has now expanded the reach of this practice by becoming a member of RSM McGladrey Network. Through this association, HLB is affiliated with more than 140 other independent accounting and consulting firms located across the country and around the world, and is able to serve clients wherever they conduct business. HLB's audit practice is subject to peer review by outside professionals and to review by the Public Company Accounting Oversight Board (PCAOB). While such oversight is not required for the work HLB does with most of its clients, it provides a statement for clients that HLB meets or exceeds professional standards.

Contributing to Chattanooga

HLB is committed to supporting enterprises that help Chattanooga grow and enhance its quality of life. The firm considers that the city's ability to provide for the neediest of its citizens is a yardstick of its greatness, and so it supports—both philanthropically and in its work in serving clients—many of the community's nonprofit organizations. As a growing city, Chattanooga also needs able contractors, and HLB is pleased to be helping more and more of these firms with accounting, technology, and other services that they need to prosper.

Giving enterprises the tools they need to flourish is one reason HLB has been around for so long and the reason it will continue to be a leader in its field for another 60 years and beyond.

Above left: Each of Hazlett, Lewis & Bieter's staff members specializes in a particular field to best serve clients. Shown here are (left to right): Rhonda Griffith, Warren McEwen, Becky Fingerle, and Andrew Glenn. Above right: The company's operations are located at Market Court in Chattanooga.

Joseph Decosimo and Company, PLLC

This nationally recognized regional accounting firm with offices in Tennessee, Georgia, Ohio, and the Cayman Islands provides assurance, litigation support, and corporate finance services, as well as international and domestic tax services, to public and private corporations in nearly every industry.

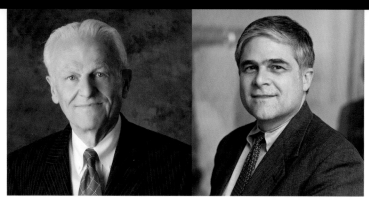

Above: Joe Decosimo (shown left) cofounded the firm of Joseph Decosimo and Company, PLLC in 1971 in Chattanooga, Tennessee. His son Nick Decosimo (shown right) is managing principal of the firm.

For more than 30 years, Joseph Decosimo and Company, PLLC has helped clients maximize value with a wide range of financial and business advisory services. The firm was founded on the values of honesty, integrity, respect, and objectivity, which have made Decosimo a trusted name across the Southeast and beyond. Decosimo considers these values to be key to a successful client relationship and relevant from Main Street to Wall Street.

Headquartered in Chattanooga since it was founded in 1971, Decosimo has grown from a local accounting practice to a nationally recognized regional firm with more than 250 professionals who serve clients in virtually every industry,

offering assurance, tax, corporate finance, and litigation support services. Today the firm has offices in Chattanooga, Knoxville, Memphis, and Nashville, Tennessee; Atlanta and Dalton, Georgia; Cincinnati, Ohio; and the Cayman Islands.

Decosimo's Support of Clients

Decosimo continues to emerge as a leading alternative to the Big Four accounting firms in the Southeast, especially for midsize companies that require a high level of expertise but appreciate the extra attention that a client-focused regional firm can offer.

Ranging from small, closely held businesses and partnerships to larger midsize companies with revenues exceeding $1.5 billion, Decosimo clients benefit from working with a regional firm that shares their values, responds to their needs, possesses a depth of experience and resources, and maintains strong relationships with nationally recognized financial institutions.

Decosimo offers an array of professional services beyond traditional audit and tax solutions. Clients turn to Decosimo for

business valuations, international business advisory, litigation support, and fraud investigation and forensic accounting services.

Decosimo's Support of Chattanooga

The Decosimo name stands for more than exceptional professional services. The community recognizes the legacy of caring that was begun by the firm's cofounders decades ago.

Decosimo's leaders are some of the most influential philanthropists and fundraisers in their community. Cofounders Joe Decosimo, Jerry V. Adams, and Marion G. Fryar continue to serve on many nonprofit boards of directors, volunteering their time to govern and find support for organizations that are important to the success of the community. In 2006 Nick Decosimo, managing principal, chaired the United Way of Greater Chattanooga fund-raising campaign, which raised a record $11.6 million to fund vital community services. Nick was the third Decosimo family member and fourth principal of the company to lead the community campaign for the local United Way chapter.

Decosimo At A Glance

- Founded in 1971 in Chattanooga, Tennessee
- Ranked in 2006 as one of the nation's 10 fastest-growing accounting firms
- Only regional accounting firm with offices in each of Tennessee's four largest cities
- More certified public accountants (CPAs) than any other Tennessee-based accounting firm
- Over 250 professionals and staff members
- Six professionals with accredited business valuation (ABV) credentials—more than any other firm in the region
- Six certified fraud examiners

In 2005, 2006, and 2007, Fred Decosimo, principal, was named one of the most powerful people in the state, according to the Power 100 list compiled annually by *Business Tennessee* magazine. The only accounting firm executive to be named to the list, Fred Decosimo was recognized for his political fund-raising and community involvement.

Chattanooga Manufacturers Association

Focused on educating the workforce, building relationships with business and government leaders, protecting the environment, and promoting healthy competition that leads to profits and growth, this independent trade association has advocated the interests of Chattanooga manufacturers for more than 100 years.

In the early 20th century, Chattanooga became known as the Dynamo of Dixie. Foundries, textile mills, and chemical plants crowded the banks of the Tennessee River, turning out boilers, stove burners, and furniture bound for markets across the rapidly modernizing country. Shepherding the ascent of manufacturing was the Chattanooga Manufacturers Association (CMA).

This association was founded in 1902 by Captain C. D. Mitchell, a Civil War veteran and local foundryman, and it started out by helping to negotiate lower freight rates for manufacturers shipping their goods to the Midwest. Ever since then, its influence has grown. Today, the CMA stands up for Chattanooga manufacturers regarding

legislative and regulatory activities to preserve manufacturers' interests.

Empowering manufacturing empowers the city's economy. Manufacturing accounts for 15.2 percent of Chattanooga's economic base. More than 34,000 people in the city work in manufacturing—and earn wages 18 percent higher than the national average for nonmanufacturing jobs. Job opportunities in the sector exist for nearly everyone because manufacturers employ workers from across the educational spectrum—from those with a general equivalency diploma to those with a doctoral degree.

The CMA represents more than 250 members. It voices their views on

matters ranging from public policy to the environment to workforce development to energy costs. For instance, it works to ensure that public utility rates are set fairly so that there will be reliable water, natural gas, and electricity for industry at costs that enable manufacturers to remain competitive.

By the mid 20th century, industrialization in Chattanooga had established the city as a major hub for the transportation of goods—by highway, waterway, and rail. Today's manufacturers are also supported by a strong infrastructure, educational facilities, and environmental proactivism. Situated among picturesque mountain ridges, clear lakes and rivers, and dense greenery, Chattanooga has become the Scenic City. The CMA takes environmental stewardship seriously. It establishes high environmental standards for manufacturers and raises awareness, and its members meet or exceed Clean Air Act standards. The CMA's work bolsters Chattanooga as a wonderful place in which to locate a company.

The CMA pays dividends to manufacturers in many ways. The CMA refers

business opportunities to its members and facilitates their working together as partners in the city's progress. It helps members build alliances with business, professional, and government leaders in the region. CMA presents seminars on matters such as the nuances of workers' compensation, media interaction, labor relations, and compliance with government regulations.

Today manufacturers in Chattanooga are creating technological innovations for traditional production as well as next-generation industries—such as robotics for automotive assembly, advanced medical devices, nanotechnology-enhanced goods, and full automation for wind-tower production. Foreign markets import more and more of these goods, helping the United States to balance trade. And helping Chattanooga manufacturers contribute to this balance, the CMA fosters a business community in which its members can flourish.

Additional information can be found on the Chattanooga Manufacturers Association's Web site at www.cma1902.com.

Above left: The 1925 board of governors of the Chattanooga Manufacturers Association (CMA) meets at the home of CMA founder Captain C. D. Mitchell (shown ninth from left, gentleman with a beard, wearing a vest). Above right, both photos: CMA hosts the 3M Visiting Wizards, who encourage young people to become interested in science and technology by providing interesting educational demonstrations and hands-on experiments, as they visit local elementary schools.

PROFILES OF COMPANIES AND ORGANIZATIONS
Utilities and Telecommunications

Communications, Inc.

For 'the Comcast community, it is not just about cable; it is all about connecting'—connecting people to information, entertainment, and each other in one community and around the world. Connecting helps weave the fabric of modern society, and Comcast is in the business of making it all possible.

Comcast Cable Communications, Inc.—one of the largest providers of cable products and services in the United States—was established in 1963. A handful of entrepreneurs purchased a 1,200-subscriber cable system in Tupelo, Mississippi, mainly to help people in remote areas receive a better broadcast signal. Currently, Comcast hosts 24 million cable customers, one million high-speed Internet customers, and two million voice customers in 39 states and Washington, D.C.

Today Comcast offers video, online, and voice products and services. The company also develops, manages, and operates broadband cable networks and delivers programming to its subscribers.

Chattanooga's Comcast

Comcast's Chattanooga history began in 1976 when Chattanooga Cable TV Company obtained nonexclusive franchises for the cities of Chattanooga, East Ridge, and Red Bank. In 1996 Comcast purchased the cable television business of the E. W. Scripps Company, the parent company of the Chattanooga Cable TV Company, and in 1997

Chattanooga Cable TV's name was changed to Comcast Communications.

Comcast serves the greater Chattanooga area, Athens, and portions of north Georgia, employing approximately 300 people locally.

Comcast in the Community

For Comcast, empowering its communities and enriching lives is just as important as giving its customers the most innovative entertainment and communication services available. As of 2006, The Comcast Foundation has contributed more than $30 million to nonprofit organizations across the United States. Founded in 1999, The Comcast Foundation supports literacy and learning programs, volunteerism projects and initiatives, scholarships to those in need, and community partnerships.

In addition, Chattanooga's Comcast supports numerous local nonprofit organizations in many ways. Comcast's most recent contributions and sponsorships include the following:

- **The Market Street Bridge:** More than just a steel and concrete ribbon that spans the Tennessee River between downtown Chattanooga and the North Shore District, the Market Street Bridge, a Chattanooga architectural treasure, is Tennessee's only drawbridge, and one of only a handful of drawbridges in the United States. In a dramatic display of a drawbridge in action, the Market Street Bridge's spans were joined in August 2007 to signify its grand reopening after two years of renovation. At the grand reopening event, sponsors, including Comcast, and attendees traversed the newly restored bridge.

- **A Night to Remember:** What began in the mid 1980s as a grassroots effort to raise scholarship money with a Black College Football Classic has grown into an entertainment extravaganza that attracts 4,500 people each year and has raised more than $4 million to help cultivate the young minds of Chattanooga children, changing lives forever. More than 4,000 students have directly benefited from A Night to Remember through scholarships, intervention programs, and cultural enrichment. Comcast is proud to be a presenting sponsor.

- **Comcast First Day Festival:** When moms, dads, and kids get together at the Comcast First Day Festival at the Chattanooga Zoo to kick off the new school year, the place really becomes a zoo! In 2007 Comcast hosted the 5th Annual First Day Festival. This always-popular free event provides age-appropriate activities, including information and giveaways from a variety of social

This page, above: A lobby wall displays Comcast Cable Communications, Inc.'s video, Internet, and phone services. Opposite page: Comcast is dedicated to providing exceptional customer service for all of the products and services it offers. Shown here is a Comcast customer service center.

Above, both photos:
Comcast continually brings
its customers the most
advanced technologies in
communications media.
The Comcast Triple Play
package includes Comcast
Digital Cable with Channel 1
On Demand, Comcast
High-Speed Internet, and
Comcast Digital Voice.

service agencies. A record 6,000 people attended the event in 2007, and they received helpful information about ways to keep kids healthy and to prepare them to learn.

Comcast and Public Television: Comcast improves the quality of life in the communities it serves by providing meaningful content that informs, involves, and inspires. In January 2008 Comcast entered into an exciting new partnership, advancing the cause of the local PBS Station, WTCI. This venture is Comcast's commitment to "harness the power of television and other media for the public good." The goal of the partnership is to inform, engage, enlighten, and delight viewers, to the benefit of all. Comcast is proud to be a corporate leader in supporting public television.

Comcast in Education: Comcast's Courtesy Cable TV service is provided to city and county schools, private schools, and municipal buildings in all franchised areas. More than 30 hours of airtime is provided weekly on cable Channel 3 for the University of Tennessee at Chattanooga and for Chattanooga State Technical Community College programming. Education Showcase, a 30-minute program for educators, is also aired on cable Channel 3.

Additional recipients of Comcast's sponsorships and support include

- Chattanooga Kids Expo, a two-day event that highlights children's nutrition and health, educational tools, entertainment, and books;
- Friday Night Live, an event for community teenagers that features performances by local talent in a safe and secure environment;
- the Ronald McDonald House Children's Festival;
- the National Association for the Advancement of Colored People (NAACP);
- the Chattanooga Area Chamber of Commerce;
- the local United Way;

- Allied Arts;
- First Things First;
- Signal Centers, Inc.;
- Junior Achievement;
- the City of Chattanooga's education, arts, and culture programs; and
- the Chattanooga Area Food Bank.

Comcast's Complete Products and Services

Comcast is committed to bringing high quality, reliable, friendly service and more entertainment value to its customers. This company continually offers new programming and improved cable services, as well as digital, high-definition, residential, and commercial high-speed Internet service. In 2007

Comcast launched its phone service that offers unlimited local and long-distance calling. Specifically, Comcast's range of services includes the following:

- Comcast Digital Cable offers up to 250 channels, parental controls, an interactive program guide, and a growing menu of On Demand programs, which archives more than 8,000 programs per month and allows viewers to pause, rewind, and fast forward.

- For Internet service, Comcast is one of the nation's leading broadband providers. Its PowerBoost technology uses capacity already built

into its advanced fiber-optic network, making it faster than ever to download software, music, photos, and videos. The company has added 65 features to its online portal, Comcast.net, including McAfee Security, the Comcast Photo Center, Comcast Video Mail, the Comcast Fan broadband multimedia player, and a customizable toolbar that has phishing protection and a spyware scanner.

- Comcast Digital Voice is unique among phone service providers because calls originate and travel over the company's advanced proprietary managed network. Other companies use services that travel over the public domain. Comcast Digital Voice is a

digital-quality phone service that includes unlimited direct-dial local and domestic long-distance calling, competitive international rates, Internet access to voice mail, online call management, Enhanced 911 (E911) service, and 12 popular calling features.

Overall, Comcast always seeks to enhance its existing products and to introduce new products that exceed customers' expectations. Comcast Cable Communications, Inc. continues to provide new technology, new opportunities for subscribers and employees, faster Internet service, clearer broadband phone service, and innovative programming through its 15 cable networks.

Above left: Comcast delivers a full, rich complement of video, Internet, and phone services for its customers. Above right: Comcast Digital Cable offers some 250 television channels along with a continually growing archive of video-on-demand programs.

EPB

Whether working toward a greener future, helping those in need keep their critical utilities on, or giving a boost to local businesses, this publicly owned utility and telecommunications company serves 163,000 customers, reaching far and wide to make a difference in the lives of Chattanoogans.

EPB's connection to its community extends much further than its electricity and telecommunications network. Through renewable resource programs, business credit incentives, and philanthropy, the nonprofit agency is having a positive impact on Greater Chattanooga and beyond.

The Tennessee legislature created EPB in 1935 to provide Chattanooga with electricity, and in 1939 EPB transmitted electricity to its first customers—six homes in east Chattanooga. Today the publicly owned utility serves more than 163,000 customers in an area of 600 square miles that includes Greater Chattanooga and parts of surrounding counties in Tennessee and areas of north Georgia.

In 2000 EPB branched into telecommunications services for businesses, launching EPB Telecom. Three years later, it introduced an all-fiber, high-speed Internet service. EPB Telecom now offers a suite of Internet and local and long-distance telephone services.

EPB's mission to enhance the quality of life in its community has inspired the agency's business-boosting and environmentally friendly programs. Working with local, regional, state, and national economic development organizations, EPB offers qualified business customers an enhanced growth credit and a manufacturing credit, which can lead to substantial savings in power costs.

Preserving clean air and water, conserving energy, and reducing dependence on fossil fuels are important goals for EPB. In fact, EPB, along with other local public power companies, partnered with the Tennessee Valley Authority (TVA) to bring the Green Power Switch® program to Tennessee valley residents. The program produces electricity from renewable sources—such as solar energy, wind, and methane gas—to create energy that is usable in people's everyday lives. Customers can purchase blocks of this "green power." Each block of green power a customer purchases is the equivalent of planting an acre of trees, recycling 883 pounds of newspaper, or recycling 240 pounds of aluminum. The green power is added to the total power mix and shared by all customers in the Tennessee valley.

The spirit of sharing is taken to the next level by the EPB Power Share program, which allows customers to contribute directly to the monthly electricity bills of local families in need. All donated funds are handled through United Way 211—an outreach program of United Way through which 100 percent of contributed funds are distributed to qualified local families. EPB's own charitable contributions are making a difference as well. It has supported more than 150 organizations, including Habitat for Humanity, Hamilton County Schools, and the Urban League of Greater Chattanooga.

For more than 70 years, EPB has helped Chattanooga's people and economy to thrive. This commitment to the region's well-being will continue to guide EPB.

Cherbo Publishing Group

Cherbo Publishing Group's business-focused, art book–quality publications, which celebrate the vital spirit of enterprise, are custom books that are used as high-impact economic development tools to enhance reputations, increase profits, and provide global exposure for businesses and organizations.

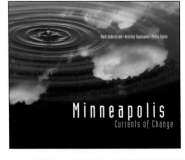

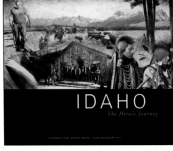

Jack Cherbo, Cherbo Publishing Group president and CEO, has been breaking new ground in the sponsored publishing business for more than 40 years.

"Previously, the cost of creating a handsome book for business developments or commemorative occasions fell directly on the sponsoring organization," Cherbo says. "My company pioneered an entirely new concept—funding these books through the sale of corporate profiles."

Cherbo honed his leading edge in Chicago, where he owned a top advertising agency before moving into publishing. Armed with a degree in business administration from Northwestern University, a mind that never stopped, and a keen sense of humor, Cherbo set out to succeed— and continues to do just that.

Cherbo Publishing Group (CPG), formerly a wholly owned subsidiary of

Jostens, Inc., a Fortune 500 company, has been a privately held corporation since 1993. CPG is North America's leading publisher of quality custom books for commercial, civic, historical, and trade associations. Publications range from hardcover state, regional, and commemorative books to softcover state and regional business reports. The company is headquartered in Encino, California, and operates regional offices in Philadelphia, Minneapolis, and Houston.

About CPG Publications

CPG has created books for some of America's leading organizations, including the U.S. Chamber of Commerce, Empire State Development, California Sesquicentennial Foundation, Chicago O'Hare International Airport, and the Indiana Manufacturers Association. Participants have included ConAgra, Dow Chemical Company, Merck & Company, and Blue Cross Blue Shield.

CPG series range from history books to economic development/relocation books and from business reports to publications of special interest. The economic development series spotlights the outstanding economic and quality-of-life advantages of fast-growing cities, counties, regions, or states. The annual business reports provide an economic snapshot of individual cities, regions, or states. The commemorative series marks milestones for corporations, organizations, and professional and trade associations.

To find out how CPG can help you celebrate a special occasion, or for information on how to showcase your company or organization, contact Jack Cherbo at 818-783-0040, extension 26, or visit www.cherbopub.com.

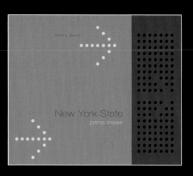

Select CPG Publications

VISIONS OF OPPORTUNITY
City, Regional, and State Series

ALABAMA *The Progress, The Promise*

AMERICA & THE SPIRIT
OF ENTERPRISE
Century of Progress, Future of Promise

CALIFORNIA *Golden Past, Shining Future*

CONNECTICUT *Chartered for Progress*

DELAWARE *Incorporating Vision in Industry*

FORT WORTH *Where the Best Begins*

GREATER PHOENIX *Expanding Horizons*

INDIANA
Crossroads of Industry and Innovation

JACKSONVILLE
Where the Future Leads

NASHVILLE *Amplified*

MICHIGAN *America's Pacesetter*

MILWAUKEE *Midwestern Metropolis*

MISSOURI *Gateway to Enterprise*

NEW YORK STATE *Prime Mover*

NORTH CAROLINA *The State of Minds*

OKLAHOMA *The Center of It All*

PITTSBURGH *Smart City*

SOUTH DAKOTA *Pioneering the Future*

TOLEDO *Access. Opportunity. Edge.*

UTAH *Life Elevated*

WESTCHESTER COUNTY, NEW YORK
Headquarters to the World

WEST VIRGINIA *Reaching New Heights*

LEGACY
Commemorative Series

ALBERTA AT 100
Celebrating the Legacy

BUILD IT & THE CROWDS WILL COME
Seventy-Five Years of Public Assembly

CELEBRATE SAINT PAUL
150 Years of History

DAYTON *On the Wings of Progress*

THE EXHIBITION INDUSTRY
The Power of Commerce

IDAHO *The Heroic Journey*

MINNEAPOLIS *Currents of Change*

NEW YORK STATE ASSOCIATION
OF FIRE CHIEFS
Sizing Up a Century of Service

ROCHESTER, MINNESOTA
An International Celebration

VIRGINIA
Catalyst of Commerce for Four Centuries

VISIONS TAKING SHAPE
*Celebrating 50 Years of the Precast/
Prestressed Concrete Industry*

ANNUAL BUSINESS REPORTS
MINNESOTA REPORT *2007*

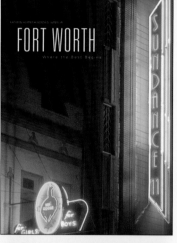
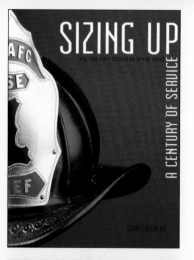
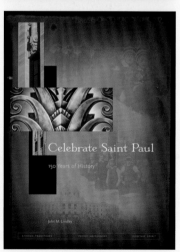
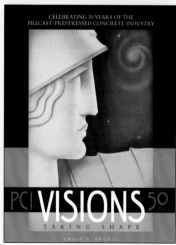
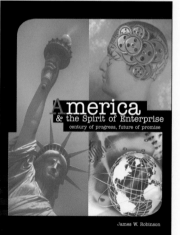

PHOTO CREDITS